THE GOLDEN DOUBLE

NORMAN GILLER
TERRY BAKER
Edited by Michael Giller

Introduced by
DAVE MACKAY
The Braveheart of Spurs

NMG

A NormanMichaelGillerPublishing publication
in association with Terry Baker, of A1 Sporting Speakers
© Norman Giller/Michael Giller/Terry Baker 2010

First published in 2010 by NMG Publishing
PO Box 3386, Ferndown, BH22 8XT

10 9 8 7 6 5 4 3 2 1

A CIP catalogue for this title is available from the British Library
ISBN 978-0-9543243-8-4
Typeset and designed by NMG Enterprises, Dorset, UK
Printed and bound in the United Kingdom by Antony Rowe Limited
Bumper's Farm, Chippenham, Wiltshire SN14 6LH

The majority of photographs in this book have been provided by premier promotions agency
A1 Sporting Speakers (www.a1sportingspeakers.com). There are also photos from the private
collections of Jimmy Greaves, Dave Mackay, Terry Baker, NMG Publishing and various photo
agencies and Tottenham supporters. Best efforts have been made to clear all copyrights.
The Art Turner illustrations are ©Art Turner 2010

THE GOLDEN DOUBLE

50 years on, the story of Tottenham's greatest season

NORMAN GILLER
TERRY BAKER
Edited by Michael Giller

Introduced by
DAVE MACKAY
The Braveheart of Spurs

NMG

Dedicated to the memories of
Bill Nicholson and **Danny Blanchflower**,
the main architects of the glorious Double Team

THE GOLDEN DOUBLE: *Contents*

Art Turner
2010

Dave Mackay, the Braveheart of Spurs, in the summertime of his life in 1961.

Kick Off by *DAVE MACKAY*

I CAN'T believe that it's fifty years since that unforgettable Double. It seems like only the day before yesterday when we were parading the FA Cup around Wembley in May 1961 to go with the League Championship trophy we had clinched at Tottenham a few weeks earlier.

Everybody had said it was the Impossible Dream, and there were a lot of raised eyebrows when our skipper Danny Blanchflower first began talking about us doing the Double even before a ball had been kicked at the start of that season. Anybody who knows me will confirm that it was not in my nature to talk about what I was going to do, but to get on and do it. But Danny was a different type of man and kept on insisting that we could do something that no team in the 20th Century had managed.

By Christmas a lot of people were believing we could achieve it. We started the season with a rush, and after we had set a record of winning our first eleven matches many good judges in the game joined Danny in saying that the Double was on.

Something magical was happening on the pitch. It was as if almost everything we touched turned to goals. We were paralysing defences with our passing movements and the finishing, particularly by big Bobby Smith and Les Allen, was dynamic. What pleased the perfectionist in me was that we were not just winning our matches but doing it with style, even a bit of a swagger.

The secret of our success was simple: team-work and team spirit. We all played for each other, and made ourselves available for the ball when attacking and made sure we picked up opponents when defending. Our manager Bill Nichsolson was a quiet yet demanding man, who always kept his feet on the floor and preached that we should keep things simple. Bill was a brutally honest man, and I think the team he built was created in his image – honest and totally focused. There was never any false praise or false hopes where Bill Nick was concerned. If you wanted success you had to EARN it.

It's impossible to talk about that season without mentioning the support we got. It was fantastic, and made us all walk a foot taller. I was involved with many clubs as player and manager during my career, but there will always be a lot of Tottenham carved into my heart. The Double season was, well, as good as it gets, and I was proud and privileged to be part of it. This book will refresh the memories of those who were there and be a magic carpet ride for younger generations who have only heard the legend. COYS!

The Stuff of Dreams by *TERRY BAKER*

LIKE all true blue-and-white blooded Spurs fans, I grew up listening to the stories of the magical Double-winning season when Tottenham achieved the Impossible Dream. It is part of our heritage, cemented into our football folklore. We were the first club of the century to do it, we led the way and we set the new sky-high standards. My love affair with Spurs started the following year when Jimmy Greaves joined the all-conquering side, but throughout the 49 years of my support I have lost count of the number of older fans who have said: "You should have been there the previous season. It was out of this world."

For a long time now I have wanted to produce a book that really captures that season, and the 50th anniversary gives me the ideal opportunity. Along with distinguished sports historian Norman Giller – who followed the team as a Fleet Street football reporter – I have ploughed through the archives to dig up every possible fact. Helping delve behind the scenes has been Michael Giller, Norman's son who is a respected sports statistician and was such a Tottenham nut in his school days that he used to sleep in the Spurs shirt given to him by Steve Perryman.

There will be other books published to mark the Golden Jubilee of the Double, but none I can assure you that can match our inside information. It has been my privilege to represent many of the surviving players from that stupendous Tottenham team, and they have given me background facts that bring an intimate touch to this tribute to – arguably – the greatest British club side of all time.

We are honoured to have the book introduced and – if you are lucky – autographed by one of the legends of The Lane, Dave Mackay, the Spurs braveheart who many considered the most vital member of that exceptional Tottenham team.

That wonderful manager Bill Nicholson went on record with the comment: "Dave Mackay was my best signing. He was such an inspirational player who could lift the players around him with his energy and enthusiasm, and he also had exceptional skill as well as power in that left foot of his."

When I asked Dave just how good the team was, he told me in that no-holds-barred way of his: "The best, particularly in the first half of the season. We had the League championship virtually wrapped up by Chritmas, and then – with Danny Blanchflower

Fifty years on: Terry Baker (centre) with veteran Double heroes Cliff Jones and Bobby Smith

giving inspired leadership – we put our minds to winning the Cup. Many outstanding sides had failed before us, but to a man we decided we could and would do it."

For a less biased view, I put the 'how good were they?' question to my mate Jimmy Greaves, who I have been privileged to manage for getting on fifteen years. Jimmy, of course, played against Spurs in that Doube year when he was a one-man goal machine for Chelsea. He told me: "You can believe all the stories you hear about them. Old timers are not exaggerating when they describe them as probably the best British club team ever. They did not have a single weakness in the side, and their midfield trio of Danny Blanchflower, John White and Dave Mackay was world class. They were perfectly balanced, with creative genius coming from Danny and John and stunning power from Dave. When I came home from Italy in the autumn of 1961 I had the pick of clubs to choose from but there was only one side I wanted to join. When Bill Nick decided to buy me it was as if Christmas had come early. I was signing for the finest club team of them all."

We hope the book reignites memories for those of you who were lucky enough to be there, and that it informs, entertains and enlightens the younger generation who have heard the tales but are not quite sure if they are true.

Here's the evidence. This is the inside story of the Golden Double. Enjoy. COYS.

W E have furnished this book with a new, compelling insight into the Double triumph by revisiting the 1960-61 season in match-by-match order, hopefully giving you a taste of what it was like to be there. Many of the eyewitness quotes I gathered during my days as a front-line Fleet Street football reporter, and others have been quarried from the memory of those who played with and against 'Super Spurs', and also those who watched with a growing excitement bordering on euphoria.

Veteran supporters inundated us with their memories, and a lot of fans from the younger generation joined in the anthem of praise for the unmatchable Tottenham side, which was magnificently marshalled by captain Danny Blanchflower and memorably managed by 'Sir' Bill Nicholson.

As Danny Boy said, "the team provided poetry in motion ..."

Brown, Baker, Henry
They roll off the tongue like old friends
Blanchflower, Norman, Mackay
Creating a legend that never ends
Jones, White, Smith
They played the game with style and flair
Allen, Dyson, Medwin
And were – at the double – beyond compare

These days, doubles and even trebles are fairly commonplace, so there is a young generation growing up who will not understand what all the fuss was about. But back then in those early, swinging 'sixties the Double was considered the Impossible Dream because it had been a bridge too far all the major clubs of the time, including the 'Big Two', Manchester United and Wolves.

A New Millennium footballer finding hmself dropped into 1960 would feel as if he had landed on another planet. They even spoke a different language in the soccerland of 1960. There were wing-halves, inside-forwards and wingers, two points for a win, and shoulder charges were allowed against unprotected, ball-bouncing goalkeepers. Fearsome defenders were allowed to tackle from behind, and words and phrases like striker, overlap, workrate, tackling back, centre-back, man-to-man marking, substitutes, red and yellow cards, and the professional foul had yet to enter the football vocabulary. Most teams played with five forwards, including two wingers who used the full width of the pitch. The most common playing formation was 2-3-5, two fullbacks, three half-backs including the centre-half and five forwards. The more progressive teams were boldly experimenting with the 4-2-4 line-up that served world champions Brazil so well in the 1958 World Cup in Sweden.

On the packed terraces they waved wooden rattles, and about the most imaginative chant that they stretched to was 'two-four-six-eight ... who do we appreciate'. These were the good old bad old days when we still had threepenny bits and tanner coins, and it cost just a couple of bob (10p) to stand on the terraces, and for an Oxford scholar (a dollar ... five shillings ... 25p) you could sit in comfort in the stand. All-seater grounds were decades away.

Floodlit football was just seeing the light of day, and Saturday was the big football day when millions would tune into Sports Report on the BBC wireless Light Programme on which Eamonn Andrews would introduce the five o'clock results and reports. Television hardly got a look in. Saturday 'Classified' evening papers – in London, the *Star, News* amd *Standard* – sold in their thousands. If you so much as mentioned Sunday professional football you were risking being thrown into the Tower during an era when the Lord's Day Observance Society was all-powerful.

It was suggested that football was going crazy because, in March 1960, a British record fee of £55,000 exchanged hands between Manchester City and Huddersfield Town. In return City got a skinny, 19-year-old Scottish goal hunter called Denis Law. He would prove worth his weight in gold (and goals).

A smell of revolution mixed with the aroma of embrocation and dubbined, ankle-high boots as the 'sixties dawned. The players were tied to a maximum £20-a-week wage, and they were ready to strike to kick away what they considered the shackles of soccer slavery. Jimmy 'The Beard' Hill, then a footballer with Fulham, was the main spokesman for the players' union.

Tottenham came into the new season on a wave of optimism after finishing third in the First Division title race in 1959-60, just two points behind champions Burnley. Danny Blanchflower was openly talking about doing the Double that 1960 FA Cup winners Wolves had just missed by a single point.

Most people dismissed it as Blanchflower blarney.

Fasten your safety belts and come with us back to August 1960. It is going to be an exhilarating and exciting ride.

Norman Giller

THE SPURS SQUAD 1960-61

Player	Born	Ht/Wt	Previous club
Bill Brown	Oct 8 1931, Arbroath	6ft 0in 12-7	Dundee
Peter Baker	Dec 10, 1931, Hampstead	5ft 9in 10-11	Enfield
Ron Henry	Aug 17 1934, Shoreditch	5ft 10in 11-13	Rebourne
Danny Blanchflower	Feb 10 1926, Belfast	5ft 9in 11-2	Aston Villa
Maurice Norman	May 8 1934, Mulbarton	6ft 1in 12-4	Norwich
Dave Mackay	Nov 14 1934, Edinburgh	5ft 7.5in 11-3	Hearts
Cliff Jones	Feb 7 1935, Swansea	5ft 7in 10-2	Swansea
John White	Apl 28 1937, Musselburgh	5ft 7.5in 10-7	Falkirk
Bobby Smith	Feb 22 1933, Lingdale	5ft 9in 13-1	Chelsea
Les Allen	Sept 4 1937, Dagenham	5ft 10in 10-2	Chelsea
Terry Dyson	Nov 29 1934, Malton	5ft 3in 9-8	Scarborough
Terry Medwin	Sept 25 1932, Swansea	5ft 9in 11-8	Swansea
Frank Saul	Aug 23 1943, Canvey Island	5ft 9in 11-6	Spurs Juniors
Tony Marchi	Jan 21 1933, Edmonton	5ft 11.5in 12-5	Spurs Juniors
John Hollowbread	Jan 2 1934, Ponders End	5ft 11in 12-4	Enfield
Ken Barton	Sept 20 1937, Caernarfon	5ft 9in 11-7	Spurs Juniors
John Smith	Jan 4 1939, Shoreditch	5ft 7in 11-1	West Ham

Manager Bill Nicholson called on 17 players during the 49-match season, with Danny Blanchflower, Ron Henry, John White and Les Allen present in all the games in what were, of course, pre-substitute days. Goalkeeper Bill Brown and centre-half Maurice Norman missed just one match, and John Hollowbread, Ken Barton and John Smith came in for one game each. In these days of enormity, it is interesting to note that Maurice Norman was the only one who stood above six foot. Even more surprising is that Dave Mackay (5ft 7 and a bit) and Bobby Smith (5ft 9in) were not the giants they appeared to be when running on to the pitch. But they stand tall in the memory.

It was during this season that the maximum £20 a week was kicked out. Even with bonuses for winning the League and the Cup, each of the 17 players earned less than £2,500 in that Double year. The following season wages went up to £65 a week. Bill Nick, a great believer in the team ethic, insisted on equal pay for all.

League Match 1: *August 20 1960*

First Division   White Hart Lane   Attendance: 50,393
TOTTENHAM 2, EVERTON 0

AN undistinguised match was into its 85th minute before Spurs scored the first goal of what was to become an historic season. Bobby Smith bullocked his way through the Everton defence and was shaping to shoot when he was unceremoniously sent tumbling just inside the 18-yard box. A chorused cry of 'Penalty' from the Spurs fans suddenly turned to cheers as Les Allen swept the loose ball into the net.

> **QUOTE – Bobby Smith**: ‘I was mouthing off to the referee that I had been fouled, but he played the advantage and Les did the business. If we had not scored then I would have felt robbed, and Everton would have got off the hook and probably nicked a point.’

Two minutes later the mighty Smith wrapped up the points for Spurs when he went down on one knee to head in a cross from John White.

It was not a performance that added weight to the pre-season predictions from Danny Blanchflower that this was going to be Tottenham's year to do the double. But what stood out for those looking for signs of things to come was the midfield supremacy of Blanchflower, White and Mackay against an Everton team reckoned to have one of the First Division's finest half-back lines.

Cliff Jones was a limping passenger for most of the second-half after a crunching tackle from Alex Parker, his former Army team-mate. "I thought we were pals," Jonesie said as he hobbled on the wing. Hard-as-nails Scot Parker replied: "Aye, we are, laddie, but just not today."

There was no feeling that this was going to be the start of the most glorious season in Spurs' history. The terse after-match verdict from Bill Nicholson: "We can and must do better."

TEAM AND SCORERS: Brown, Baker, Henry; Blanchflower, Norman, Mackay; Jones, White, Smith, Allen, Dyson. Goalscorers: Allen, Smith.

First Division Bloomfield Road Attendance: 27,656
BLACKPOOL 1, TOTTENHAM 3

BLACKPOOL, including the immortal Stanley Matthews on their right wing, were no match for a Spurs side that quickly got into its rhythm. Matthews was 46 years young, and still a wizard of dribble and soon set for a return home to Stoke and a glorious ending to his fairytale career. He was superbly marked by left-back Ron Henry, who allowed him few opportunities to show the now-you-see-me-now-you-don't-runs that had made him a footballing legend.

> **QUOTE** – Ron Henry: 'I had made a close study of the way Matthews tricked his opponents, and noticed that most defenders watched his body rather than the ball when marking him. He could throw them off balance with a dip of his shoulder or a double-foot feint, but I noticed that the ball usually stayed in the same spot. So I kept my eyes riveted on the ball, and most times managed to get a foot to it before he could gallop away. He paid me the compliment of calling me a bloody nuisance!'

Terry Dyson gave Spurs the lead in the ninth minute, and Blackpool could easily have conceded another three goals before Terry Medwin – deputising for injured Cliff Jones – made it 2-0 in the 37th minute. It was all over bar the shooting and the shouting in the 56th minute when Dyson nipped through a dazed Blackpool defence to collect his second and Tottenham's third goal.

Blackpool missed from the penalty spot before Jackie Mudie gave a flattering look to the scoreline with a goal in the dying moments of a game which had purists in the crowd purring at the subtlety and sophistication of some of the Spurs play. It was already clear that the precision passing of Blanchflower and White was going to be a key component.

TEAM AND SCORERS: Brown, Baker, Henry; Blanchflower, Norman, Mackay; Medwin, White, Smith, Allen, Dyson. Goalscorers: Dyson (2), Medwin.

League Match 3: *August 27 1960*

First Division   Ewood Park   Attendance 26,819
BLACKBURN ROVERS 1, TOTTENHAM 4

IT was back to Lancashire for what was expected to be a difficult assignment against a Blackburn team that had come out of the blocks quickly, winning their opening two games in impressive style and sharing top place in the First Division table with Spurs, Wolves and Sheffield Wednesday. It was virtually all over in 17 minutes … with Spurs rushing to a 3-0 lead that left Blackburn bewitched, bothered and bewildered – title of one of the hit songs of the era.

Bobby Smith started the dismantling of the Blackburn defence in the second minute, running on to a pass from Allen and slamming the ball past Rovers goalkeeper Bob Jones. Nine minutes later Smith struck again, rising above the Blackburn defence to head in a well-flighted, left-footed free-kick from Dave Mackay. Blackburn were in disarray, and Jones was picking the ball out of his net again in the 17th minute after Dyson had created an opening for Allen, who provided a deft finish.

Two minutes into the second-half Blanchflower, bossing the midfield like an imperious war general, set Allen away down the inside-left channel, and his precise pass was smacked into the net by the alert Dyson.

From then on Blackburn were forced to concentrate on damage-limitation, but they managed to catch Tottenham with a counter attack that produced a late consolation goal.

QUOTE – Ally MacLeod, Blackburn winger and later Scotland manager: ❛Spurs played stunning football throughout the season, and were just sensational against us. I considered that Spurs side one of the best British club teams I played against. They were a joy to behold, even when you were on the receiving end. As a Scot I'm proud to point out that it was Mackay and White who made the team tick.❜

TEAM AND SCORERS: Brown, Baker, Henry; Blanchflower, Norman, Mackay; Medwin, White, Smith, Allen, Dyson. Goalscorers: Smith (2), Allen, Dyson.

First Division   White Hart Lane   Attendance 45,684
TOTTENHAM 3, BLACKPOOL 1

THIS was Bobby Smith's match. He hammered the Seasiders with a hat-trick that took him past George Hunt's 1930s club record of 185 League and Cup goals. He might have scored more but for a series of magnificent saves by goalkeeper Tony Waiters, a Blackpool beach lifeguard.

It looked as if Spurs were in for an easy night when Smith scored his first goal in the third minute following a winger-style run down the right touchline by captain Blanchflower. But, inspired by Waiters, Blackpool bounced back with an equalizer nine minutes before half-time when Les Lee turned the ball past Bill Brown from close range.

The second-half belonged to Spurs in general and Smith in particular. He restored the lead with a reflex shot after Jimmy Armfield had cleared what looked a certain goal from Medwin off the line in the 51st minute. Barnstorming Bobby completed his hat-trick eight minutes from the end when he calmly controlled a centre from Medwin and slammed an unstoppable shot past Waiters. It was a goal that captured not only Bobby's power but also his under-rated technical ability. He was much more than just a powerhouse player. There was method mixed with the muscle.

QUOTE: Bobby Smith – ❛I had no idea the record was in sight. I am out of the old school of players who like to score goals rather than count them. But now I've got the record I think I have a great chance of adding to it, because this team is very special. We're really excited about the start we've made.❜

Spurs were sitting proudly at the top of the table with a maximum eight points from four matches, with Wolves and Sheffield Wednesday breathing down their necks a point behind.

TEAM AND SCORERS: Brown, Baker, Henry; Blanchflower, Norman, Mackay; Medwin, White, Smith, Allen, Dyson. Goalscorers: Smith (3).

Born Arbroath October 8 1931. Tottenham goalkeeper in 222 League matches between 1959 and 1965 after joining them from his local Dundee club for £16,500 during Bill Nicholson's first season as manager.

He was capped 28 times by Scotland, and wound down his career with Northampton Town and then Toronto Falcons.

Bill's career was squashed between two Lane goalkeepering legends in Ted Ditchburn and Pat Jennings, and he suffers by comparison. But in that Double year he was a masterful last line of defence, and had an intuitive understanding with Maurice Norman. It was Big Mo who often came to his rescue when Brown's positional sense on crosses was exposed.

He had been an outstanding winger at school but switched to goalkeeper after taking over between the sticks for an injured team-mate. Safe but unspectacular sums up Bill's play, which made him seem a little uninspiring when following the idolised showman, Ditchburn.

His strengths were a good pair of hands, which made him one of the best shot-stoppers in the game, and he perfected his distribution and had the ability to focus and give total concentration when the pressure on his goal was at its peak.

Throughout his career, Bill – a qualified electrician – worked on building up a printing business, eventually emigrating to Canada where he became a successful property developer. He passed on in Ontario on December 1 2004, aged 73.

First Division   White Hart Lane   Attendance: 55,442
TOTTENHAM 4, MANCHESTER UNITED 1

SEPTEMBER arrived with the football world buzzing about Tottenham. Manchester United, still rebuilding after the tragedy of the 1958 Munich air crash and struggling in the relegation zone, were completely outgunned and fortunate not to get an even bigger hiding.

Spurs were presented with a gift goal in the fifth minute. Maurice Setters committed the cardinal sin of passing across the face of his own goal. John White gratefully accepted the ball and immediately released it to Bobby Smith, who drove it firmly into the net past goalkeeper Harry Gregg.

Blanchflower, White and Mackay were in total command in midfield, and set up a series of raids that culminated with Allen making it 2-0 in the 19th minute. Maurice Norman had a rare loss of concentration and Dennis Viollett cashed in on poor marking by stealing a poached goal that was completely against the run of play.

It was the White-Allen combination that restored the two goal lead in the 69th minute, Les heading in a measured pass from the silky-smooth Scot who was establishing himself as the hidden ace in the Spurs pack. Defences just did not know how to pick him up and block his instinctive and intelligent blindside runs.

Smith wrapped it up five minutes from the end with a rasping right-foot shot after the energetic Medwin had opened up the United defence with a probing run.

QUOTE – Bill Nicholson: ⁶We have got off to a satisfying start to the season, but nobody is getting carried away. Danny made those remarks before the season started that we could win the double, but I have now stopped all that sort of talk. That is not my style. We will take each game as it comes. So far, so good.⁹

TEAM AND SCORERS: Brown, Baker, Henry; Blanchflower, Norman, Mackay; Medwin, White, Smith, Allen, Dyson. Goalscorers: Smith (2), Allen (2).

First Division   Burnden Park   Attendance: 41,565
BOLTON WANDERERS 1, TOTTENHAM 2

S PURS went a goal behind for the first time in the season against a Bolton side famed and feared for their brutal tackling. The game was just three minutes old when England winger Doug Holden drifted past Peter Baker to create a chance for Billy McAdams, who had the impossible job of trying to fill the boots of Bolton legend Nat Lofthouse. He thrilled the crowd by banging the ball into the Tottenham net Lofty-style.

For a change, Spurs were not monopolizing in midfield, where Bolton schemer Freddie Hill was playing a blinder. Ray Parry hit the Tottenham bar, Hill put a shot wide when he was well placed and then Bill Brown was forced to make two excellent saves from McAdams.

Spurs were missing the drive of injured Bobby Smith, even though his 17-year-old stand-in Frank Saul was playing his heart out. The pendulum of play dramtically swayed Tottenham's way when Bolton full-back Tommy Banks was carried off with a torn thigh muscle. Suddenly the ten-man home side was having to battle to hold on to their slender lead, and when goalkeeper Eddie Hopkinson failed to collect a floated centre from White on the right wing Allen was perfectly placed to head the equalizer.

A man short in these pre-substitute days, Bolton were now struggling to hold a suddenly resurgent Spurs and the inevitable winner came when schemer White turned scorer, hooking a Blanchflower centre wide of Hopkinson and into the net in the 80th minute.

QUOTE – Danny Blanchflower: ‘I feel privileged to be skippering this team. There is a confidence and camaraderie that bodes well. I have been asked to keep my trap shut on the subject of the Double, but let me just state the blindingly obvious by saying that we could not have made a better start to the season.’

TEAM AND SCORERS: Brown, Baker, Henry; Blanchflower, Norman, Mackay; Medwin, White, Saul, Allen, Dyson. Goalscorers: Allen, White.

First Division   Highbury   Attendance: 59,868
ARSENAL 2, TOTTENHAM 3

FIFTY years on there are veteran Tottenham supporters who still claim that this was the greatest North London derby that they have witnessed. It was a see-sawing game in which the Gunners did their best to shoot down their high-riding neighbours.

Spurs had two narrow escapes as Arsenal opened with an all-out assault, and it was against the run of play when fledgling Frank Saul came of age with his first goal. He pounced on a loose ball in the 12th minute and lashed it into the net. Ten minutes later he played a part in goal number two, nodding on a Dave Mackay throw-in for Terry Dyson to head past goalkeeper Jack Kelsey.

Just when Tottenham appeared to be coasting to a record seventh straight victory, Arsenal pulled level soon after the hour with two goals in four minutes. David Herd deceived Bill Brown with a dipping shot following a Danny Clapton corner, and then Gerry Ward equalised with a speculative shot from 35 yards that sneaked past Brown through a forest of legs and into the net.

The near 60,000 crowd, with many locked out, were dismayed (Arsenal) or delighted (Spurs) when Blanchflower sliced open the Gunners defence with an exquisite through ball for Les Allen to steer in the winning goal in the 71st minute.

QUOTE – Frank Saul: "I will never forget my first goal for Spurs. To score it at Highbury was a bonus. It has made all my daily journeys to and from my home on Canvey Island worthwhile."

Blackpool lost 1-0 to Bolton in an experimental first live TV broadcast of a League match. What a pity the cameras were not at Highbury to capture this classic.

TEAM AND SCORERS: Brown, Baker, Henry; Blanchflower, Norman, Mackay; Medwin, White, Saul, Allen, Dyson. Goalscorers: Saul, Dyson and Allen.

Born Hampstead, London, December 10 1931. Played 299 League games for Spurs, and scored three goals. Signed for Tottenham from Enfield in 1952 at the age of 20, during the Arthur Rowe era and served the club for nearly 14 years.

After eventually losing his place in defence to Cyril Knowles (who was more comfortable on the left), he wound down his career in South Africa with Durban City.

Peter, educated in Arsenal territory at Southgate County School, made his debut in 1953 behind Bill Nicholson in the Spurs push-and-run team, but his early promise faded and it was five years before he established himself as regular right-back.

His solid, no-nonsense style was greatly appreciated by Danny Blanchflower, whose appetite for attack meant he often left gaping holes behind him.

He was the only member of Tottenham's magnificent defence during that Double year who was not rewarded with an international cap. Peter was unlucky to be playing when class right-backs like Jimmy Armfield, Don Howe and Mick McNeil were establishing themselves.

Art Turner 2010

Peter had the tough challenge of inheriting the No 2 Spurs shirt worn by the majestic Alf Ramsey. He did not manage to fill it at first, but by the time the Double season came round he was an assured and determined right-back who never ever let the team down.

Peter later had a successful spell in Durban as a player and then manager.

First Division   White Hart Lane   Attendance: 43,559
TOTTENHAM 3, BOLTON WANDERERS 1

FOR the second time, Spurs had to come from behind to maintain their sensational start to the season. Bolton shocked them with a seventh minute goal by Billy McAdams under the White Hart Lane lights in a match that developed into an ill-tempered affair.

Fit-again Bobby Smith equalized after 24 minutes following creative approach work by Blanchflower and Cliff Jones.

Most neutral fans thought the referee was harsh to award Spurs a penalty in the 65th minute after Terry Dyson had gone over in the penalty area. Was he pushed or did he fall? The Bolton defenders were fuming as Blanchflower coolly slotted home the spot-kick.

Bolton, perhaps understandably, became sulky and spiteful as they tried to get back into the game. Right winger Brian Birch was twice booked by the referee in an era when you almost had to commit grievous bodily harm to get sent off. Goalkeeper Eddie Hopkinson came close to getting his marching orders when he twice refused to take a goal-kick because of the abuse he was getting from the Tottenham fans baying at him from behind his net.

With the Bolton players losing their tempers, Tottenham kept focused and composed and clinched their eighth successive victory when Bobby Smith forced the ball home during a goalmouth scramble in the 85th minute.

QUOTE: – Terry Dyson: 'I did not dive. Anybody who knows me will tell you that is not my way. Somebody pushed me from behind and I went flying. The referee had a good view of it and decided to award a penalty. Bolton were upset, but that's football. The only thing that mattered to us was keeping up our winning streak.'

TEAM AND SCORERS: Brown, Baker, Henry; Blanchflower, Norman, Mackay; Jones, White, Smith, Allen, Dyson. Goalscorers: Smith (2), Blanchflower (pen).

First Division   Filbert Street   Attendance: 30,129
LEICESTER CITY 1, TOTTENHAM 2

AS well as Frank Saul did in his stand-in role, it was a huge boost to Tottenham's hopes of maintaining their blistering start to the season when Bobby Smith proved he was back to full fitness. He was playing better than at any time in his career, and his alliance with Les Allen was developing into the most potent partnership in the First Division. Both had arrived at White Hart Lane from Stamford Bridge, where they had been considered surplus to requirements. It gave each of them an extra desire to prove Chelsea wrong.

It was Smith who gave Tottenham the lead against Leicester at Filbert Street with a typical wham-bang-no-nonsense goal in the 18th minute, but Howard Riley quickly equalized with a snap shot that caught the unsighted Brown unawares.

The Smith-Allen tandem team was proving a handful for the Leicester defence and they caved in under a two-pronged assault in the 54th minute that finished with Smith slotting in his second goal. From then on Tottenham shut up shop, keeping the ball away from Leicester with precise passing movements instigated by Blanchflower and White.

Spurs had now equalled Hull City's all-time League record of nine successive victories set under the baton of Raich Carter back in 1948.

QUOTE – Les Allen: 'Bobby and I had a sort of instinctive understanding of knowing where to be to get the best out of each other. We could do no wrong in that Double season, and our confidence was sky-high. Both of us considered ourselves lucky to be getting such great service from our marvellous midfield players and from either wing. Bobby and I scored most of the goals, but it was very much a team effort.'

TEAM AND SCORERS: Brown, Baker, Henry; Blanchflower, Norman, Mackay; Medwin, White, Smith, Allen, Dyson. Goalscorers: Smith (2).

First Division   White Hart Lane Attendance   61,356
TOTTENHAM 6, ASTON VILLA 2

FRANK McGHEE, highly respected football writer on the *Daily Mirror*, had dubbed Tottenham 'Super Spurs,' a nickname that caught on with the supporters and the newspaper headline writers. They were more like supersonic in this 6-2 thrashing of Aston Villa in front of a euphoric, jam-packed 61,000-plus crowd that was shoehorned into white hot White Hart Lane.

John White started the rout in the sixth minute when he put the finishing touch to a sweeping four-man passing movement launched deep in Tottenham territory by Peter Baker. By the time the match was 30 minutes old Spurs were virtually home and dry, taking their lead to 4-0. White added a second, Smith was on hand to net number three after harassed goalkeeper Nigel Sims had dropped a whiplash left-foot shot from Dave Mackay and Dyson scored a neat goal after being put clear by the hyperactive White.

The fifth goal came early in the second-half when Dyson and White combined to create an opening for the bang-in-form Les Allen. Much to the annoyance of Bill Nicholson, Spurs took their foot off the accelerator and allowed Villa a brief respite during which they saved a little face with goals from Jimmy MacEwan and Gerry Hitchens.

Spurs saved the best for last. The ball moved on a 40-yard conveyor belt of passes in the 85th minute from Ron Henry, to Dave Mackay, on to Les Allen, out to Terry Dyson and then back to Mackay, who blasted in a full bloodied volley; a reminder that Dave was a stunning striker of the ball.

QUOTE – Nigel Sims, Villa goalkeeper: ❛This is as good an attacking team as I have faced. No wonder they have notched up ten wins on the trot. It is going to take a very special side to stop them.❜

TEAM AND SCORERS: Brown, Baker, Henry; Blanchflower, Norman, Mackay; Medwin, White, Smith, Allen, Dyson. Scorers: White 2, Mackay, Smith, Allen, Dyson.

Master manager Bill Nicholson earned the full respect of his players, as this collection of quotes – many of them as uttered 50 years ago – prove:

BILL BROWN: 'Bill was always a fair and trusting manager, and I was grateful for his support and faith when I first arrived from Dundee. It was not easy following in the steps of Ted Ditchburn, who was a legend at White Hart Lane. It took me time to win over the fans, but Bill used to quietly tell me that he had every confidence in me. For a man who had never been a goalie, he was extremely knowledgeable about the pressures and problems of the job. He used to work closely with me on training sessions to help me improve my positioning and my distribution. He was a great believer in launching counter attacks with a well placed ball from the penalty area. All right, I know I was not as exciting to watch as the acrobatic Ted Ditchburn, but we were different-style goalkeepers. Bill put me at my ease by telling me to play it my way.'

PETER BAKER: 'When I made my debut for Spurs back in 1953, Bill Nick was my team-mate. He gave me advice that helped me get my game right after a bit of an inconsistent spell. I had taken over the No 2 shirt from Alf Ramsey, who was one of the finest full-backs ever to play for England. I was in awe of Alf and modelled my early playing style on his. Bill took me to one side in training one day and told me, "Stop trying to play like Alf. He was a one-off. Be yourself." From then on my game improved so much that Bill made me a regular member of the defence when he became manager.'

RON HENRY: 'It was legend when I signed for Spurs after my National Service how Bill Nick and Alf Ramsey were always eaten up with talking tactics, and it was obvious they would both follow managerial careers. Amazingly they both became among the greatest managers of all time. Bill was a serious, deep-thinking man who had tunnel vision. All he could think of was football, football, football. He was quite strict, but if you gave him 100 per cent he treated you with respect. But he would come down like a ton of bricks on any player who did not work flat out for the team. Bill always thought the team was above any individual, and had no time for shirkers.'

Bill Nicholson, The Master Manager of White Hart Lane

DANNY BLANCHFLOWER: 'It's written in blood that Bill and I did not hit it off immediately when he became manager, and I asked for a transfer when he left me kicking my heels in the reserves. But once we put differences to one side and talked face-to-face and heart-to-heart we realised we both wanted the same thing, and that was a team that played with spirit and style. We not only got to understand each other but also to like each other, and you will be hard pushed to find a manager with greater vision and conviction. He gave me the freedom to be more than just a coin-tossing captain and by working in tandem we got the best results for Tottenham. There had been criticism from the directors early in my career at Spurs when I made tactical decisions on the pitch, but Bill understood my motives and encouraged me.'

MAURICE NORMAN: 'I was first bought from Norwich as right-back following the retirement of Alf Ramsey, but I was never really comfortable in the position. With my long legs I needed time to get into my stride, which could make it difficult for me when marking any of the many nippy wingers who were around in those days. When Bill became the coach at the end of his playing career he argued for me to be the first-choice centre-half, and he taught me a lot about positioning and the correct way to tackle. He was a master tactician and liked nothing better than being in a tracksuit out on the training ground with us. He always said that playing was the best time of your life, and that you are a long time retired. Bill had been there, done that, and had a wisdom from which we all learned.'

DAVE MACKAY: 'Bill Nicholson was my sort of guy. No bullshitting or stealing the limelight. He always called it as it was. If we played badly, he let us know in no uncertain terms. If we played well, he would make us keep our feet on the ground. He was never one to give false praise. If he said 'well done' that was worth an hour's applause. Even when we seemed to be running away with the League championship in the Double year he kept warning us not to take anything for granted. Yes, he could be miserable at times, but I know from later experience that this comes with the territory of managing a club. There are so many different problems to deal with, and on the whole Bill handled it all brilliantly. I would call him a man's manager.'

CLIFF JONES: ‘We laid the foundation for the Double on the training ground at Cheshunt. Bill was a tracksuit manager and a fanatic about perfecting tactics, and used to work us into the ground until he got his ideas across. Coaching was always his first priority and he liked to keep things simple and uncomplicated, but he would not let us go until he was convinced we had understood his theories. Danny would often pipe up with something alternative and it would be argued out until we knew exactly what was wanted. There have been few better British coaches in history than Bill Nick, who always had a clear vision of the way the game could and should be played.’

JOHN WHITE: ‘The Boss was typically thorough in the way he went about signing me. He talked to many of the players who were my team-mates at club and Army level, and rang his Scottish contacts. Bill admitted that he was worried as to whether I had the stamina and strength for English First Division football, but he relaxed when he found out I was the best cross-country runner in our battalion. People often get misled by the fact that I look quite frail, then get a surprise when they find I can run all day. I quickly struck up an understanding with Danny Blanchflower and Dave Mackay, and I am proud to be part of the best midfield trio in the League.’

BOBBY SMITH: ‘Bill Nick and I had a few up-and-a-downs over silly things, but I never lost my respect for the man. He always showed concern for me when I used to come off the pitch battered and bruised, and really appreciated my determination to carry on playing despite the aches and pains. I never really wanted to leave Chelsea, but made up my mind to show Ted Drake he was wrong when he said I wasn’t going to make it. In Bill we had the ideal thinking manager to get the most out of our team of many talents. He kept a bit of a distance between the players and himself, which is normal but he was always there for us if we needed to talk.’

LES ALLEN: ‘As somebody who had been an apprentice at Fords in Dagenham, the thought of being part of one of the greatest club teams ever was a distant dream. There was not a weakness in our side, and Bill Nick was always a manager who earned the

respect of his players with his dedicated and demanding approach. Bobby Smith and I really hit it off, and our confidence was sky high in every match we played together in that incredible season. Bill always put the emphasis on attack, and we got great support from midfield where Danny, John and Dave were magnificent. I was very pleased they were with us and not against us!'

TERRY DYSON: 'While I usually wore the No 11 shirt, Bill Nick encouraged me to play a roaming role and I used to pop up in all sorts of positions to help surprise the opposition. Defences just didn't know how to handle us, with Bobby and Les bombing through the middle, Cliffie or sometimes Terry speeding down the right, and Danny, John and Dave motoring through from midfield. Everything was geared to scoring goals, and it was Bill Nick's tactical planning that made it all easier. The two goals I scored in the European Cup Winners' Cup final in 1963 gave Bill almost as much pleasure as me. He liked to see his players enjoying their success.'

TERRY MEDWIN: 'I did not play as often as I would have liked, but I was proud and privileged to be part of one of the finest squad of players ever gathered by one club. The team had Bill Nicholson written all over it, and it was fabulous to be on the pitch when they were going flat out. I got on famously with Bill, who was one of the most conscientious and caring managers in the game. There was friendly rivalry for the wing positions but it never turned into bad blood. In Bill's shoes I would also have picked Cliff ahead of me. We grew up in Swansea together and he developed into a truly world-class player. They were memorable days, and Bill was a great manager.'

FRANK SAUL: 'Bill Nick signed me for Spurs on my seventeenth birthday and just a couple of weeks later showed great faith in me by putting me into the first-team for my League debut. His belief was that if you were good enough you were old enough. That was a fantastic squad of players, and I felt honoured to be understudying Bobby Smith who was in fabulous form. Just think, my first season as a professional and there I was part of the squad that won the Double. The Boss was always encouraging, and I felt so pleased to be able to repay him with a goal in the 1967 FA Cup final win over Chelsea.'

League Match 11: October 1 1960

First Division   Molineux   Attendance 52,829
WOLVES 0, TOTTENHAM 4

IT is estimated that at least half of the crowd had left Molineux by the time Spurs wrapped up their record eleventh successive victory. The Wolves fans just could not stomach watching their team – League champions in 1957-58 and 1958-59 and narrowly missing the Double in 1959-60 – being ripped apart by rampant Tottenham.

The Wolves goal had survived three close shaves before Cliff Jones gave Spurs the lead in the 32nd minute when he turned in a perfectly placed cross from Les Allen. A second goal seemed inevitable as the Wolves defence, missing the steadying influence of the recently retired Billy Wright, buckled under an attacking onslaught. Terry Dyson squandered two golden chances before Danny Blanchflower made it 2-0 with a long-range shot in the 44th minute.

John White fashioned goal number three in the 52nd minute, feigning as if to pass before making a sudden dash down the right wing. His cross left Allen with a simple tap-in. The energetic Dyson might have had a hat-trick, but had to settle just for the fourth and final goal in the 79th minute after a scorching shot from Bobby Smith had hit a post.

This was a victory for polished, along-the-ground football in the best Tottenham traditions over the kick-and-rush route-one style that had served Wolves so well over the previous decade. Even the hard-to-please Bill Nicholson acknowledged afterwards that he was delighted with a performance that touched the peaks of perfection.

QUOTE – Stan Cullis, legendary Wolves manager: ʻOn the evidence of this display, I would have to say that this Tottenham team is even more impressive than the Push-and-Run side of ten years ago. Bill Nicholson is a manger who deserves any success that comes to him.ʼ

TEAM AND SCORERS: Brown, Baker, Henry; Blanchflower, Norman, Mackay; Jones, White, Smith, Allen, Dyson. Goalscorers: Jones, Blanch-flower, Allen, Dyson

First Division   White Hart Lane   Attendance: 58,916
TOTTENHAM 1, MANCHESTER CITY 1

TOTTENHAM's remarkable winning streak finally came to an unsatisfactory end in a crescendo of controversy. The game against Manchester City was postponed until the Monday evening because of the Northern Ireland-England international in Belfast on the Saturday (Bobby Smith scored on his debut playing alongside young Jimmy Greaves in a 5-2 victory over an outclassed Irish side led valiantly by Danny Blanchflower).

Smith carried on where he left off in Belfast, heading Tottenham into a 27th minute lead against a Manchester City side that unashamedly set out to try to snatch a draw with a defensive formation. They packed in numbers around goalkeeper Bert Trautmann, the former German POW who was the greatest foreign-born goalkeeper ever to play in the League until the arrival decades later of Peter Schmeichel.

It was the most one-sided match witnessed at The Lane for years, with Tottenham unleashing 40 shots to the nine by City. The corner count was 14 to Spurs and two to City.

City's nine shots included one from winger Clive Colbridge in the second-half that flew beyond Bill Brown's despairing dive and into the net. Referee Gilbert Pullin appeared to be one of the few people in the ground who did not spot that Colbridge had brought the ball under control with his hand before shooting. There was uproar and to this day veteran Tottenham players and fans claim the goal should have been ruled out.

QUOTE – Danny Blanchflower: ❛All good things come to an end, but it was exasperating to lose our unbeaten record to a goal that should not have been allowed. The fact is, though, that we missed too many chance, and so we got our just desserts.❜

TEAM AND SCORERS: Brown, Baker, Henry; Blanchflower, Norman, Mackay; Medwin, White, Smith, Allen, Dyson. Goalscorers: Smith.

First Division   City Ground   Attendance 37,248
NOTTINGHAM FOREST 0, TOTTENHAM 4

FOR the only time in the season, Bill Nicholson was missing from the sidelines because of a heavy cold. His team gave him the best possible tonic with what many good judges considered their finest performance of the season. Ralph Finn, *Sunday People* reporter and a football statistician specialising in the history of Spurs, gave every player a perfect 10 out of 10 in his team ratings, the only time this had ever been achieved.

Tottenham purred to a 3-0 lead in the opening 24 minutes. Les Allen and Terry Dyson exchanged passes in the seventh minute before bringing John White into their ploy, and he neatly steered the ball into the net with the Forest defenders waiting for him to return the ball to Dyson. The second goal came in the 12th minute when under-pressure centre-half Bob McKinlay turned a Dave Mackay cross into his own net. Cliff Jones added a third in the 24th minute after Smith had won the ball with an aerial challenge.

The second-half developed into almost an exhibition match, with the Forest defenders chasing shadows. The only surprise is that all of Tottenham's pressure produced only one more goal when Jones ran on to a chipped pass from Mackay's educated left foot and scored his second goal to mark a successful return after injury.

Tottenham goakeeper Bill Brown had only one shot to save throughout the 90 minutes.

QUOTE – Bob McKinlay. Forest skipper: ‘We felt lucky to get off the pitch without conceding double figures. They might as well have given Tottenham the League championship there and then. I couldn't see how any team was gong to stop them. There was not a single weakness in the side.’

TEAM AND SCORERS: Brown, Baker, Henry; Blanchflower, Norman, Mackay; Jones, White, Smith, Allen, Dyson. Goalscorers: White, McKinlay (og), Jones (2).

Born Shoreditch, August 17 1934, one of twin brothers. Played 247 League matches for Tottenham between 1954 and 1965 before becoming a highly regarded youth coach.

He was at left-back in all 42 of Tottenham's League matches in the 1960-61 season. Capped once, in Sir Alf Ramsey's first match as England manager against France in 1963.

A skilful outside-left with Redbourne, he was spotted by Jimmy Anderson while playing for the Army team that also featured Terry Dyson. Tottenham converted him to a utility defender and he made his League debut at centre-half against Huddersfield in 1955. It was not until the 1959-60 season that he took over the No 3 shirt from Welsh international Mel Hopkins, and from then on he developed as one of the finest left-backs in the League.

Art Turner
2010

Ron perfected the art of the sliding tackle, and became a master of distribution. One of his strengths was a willingness to support Dave Mackay in foraging runs in the days before overlapping full-backs became a common sight.

He was unlucky to carry the can for England's 5-2 defeat by France in Alf Ramsey's debut match as team manager.

His long-running partnership with Peter Baker was a hugely important part of Tottenham's glory-glory march, and this likeable man later imparted his great knowledge to a procession of White Hart Lane youth players. They could not have been in better hands.

First Division   St James' Park   Attendance 51,369
NEWCASTLE UNITED 3, TOTTENHAM 4

A seven-goal thriller – following a week off because of an international weekend – was riddled with mistakes and filled with breathtaking attacking football from both sides. The two Whites on the pitch – Len for Newcastle and John for Spurs – were both prominent as the teams went at each other like heavyweight boxers determined to score a knockout while leaving their chins exposed.

It was Len White who gave the Geordies the lead in the 33rd minute, tricking his way past two defenders to score after accepting a pass from the gifted Welsh international Ivor Allchurch.

Two minutes later goalkeeper Bryan Harvey missed a cross from Terry Dyson and Maurice Norman was on hand to head an equalizer. Just sixty seconds later, hero Norman became villain when he miscued an attempted clearance and White slotted the loose ball home.

QUOTE: – Maurice Norman: ‘For the first time in the season we went into the dressing-room trailing at the interval, and we expected a rollocking from the Boss. But Bill Nick surprised us by saying that we were playing well and to keep doing what we were doing and it would come right in the second-half.’

Spurs pulled level almost immediately after the interval when goalkeeper Harvey pushed the ball into John White's path, and then in the 58th minute Cliff Jones – looking a yard off-side – made it 3-2, much to the anger of the Newcastle players and fans.

Four minutes later Gordon Hughes sent over a hopeful cross, and was as shocked as everybody else when the usually so reliable Bill Brown missed it completely and watched it drop into his net. Bobby Smith saved Bill's blushes when he converted a Les Allen cross in the 86th minute.

TEAM AND SCORERS: Brown, Baker, Henry; Blanchflower, Norman, Mackay; Jones, White, Smith, Allen, Dyson. Goalscorers: Norman, White, Jones, Smith.

Danny Blanchflower, captain marvel for Tottenham and Northern Ireland

An appreciation of *DANNY BLANCHFLOWER*
By Jimmy Greaves

GOALMASTER Jimmy Greaves played against Tottenham in their Double Year and was a member of the team the following season. Here, exclusively for our book and No 4 in the Spurs Heroes Profile series, he gives a personal assessment of skipper Danny Blanchflower:

Born Belfast, February 10 1926
Died London December 9 1993, aged 67
Career span: 1946-1963
Clubs: Glentoran, Barnsley 1949-51 (68 League games, 2 goals); Aston Villa 1951-54 (148 League games, 10 goals); Tottenham 1954-63 (337 League games, 15 goals)
Club honours: League and FA Cup winning double captain 1960-61; FA Cup winning captain 1962; European Cup-Winners' Cup captain 1963
Northern Ireland: 56 caps (2 goals)
Twice Footballer of the Year 1958 and 1961

I WAS fortunate enough to play with some of the finest footballers ever to cross the white line, but nobody had quite the same impact and influence on me as Danny Blanchflower. He always talked such good sense that I used to feel as if I were sitting at his feet taking it all in. We named our eldest son after him, and Danny was his Godfather. That's how close I was to the Irish genius.

Danny was the poet of the Sixties 'Super Spurs'. He gave the team style and panache, and was a captain in every sense of the word, inspiring the players around him with his almost arrogant performances while lifting them with words of wisdom. His contribution to the team was every bit as important as that of our outstanding manager Bill Nicholson.

His influence went much farther and deeper than his displays on the pitch. He was the dressing-room tactician, the training-ground theorist, the man who talked up for players during moments of crisis and misunderstanding.

Danny rivalled even my England team-mate Johnny Haynes for firing a killer pass through the heart of a defence, and to see him playing in tandem for Northern Ireland with the midfield maestro Jimmy McIlroy was truly poetry in motion.

Apart perhaps from Bobby Moore, I did not play with a better reader of the game than Danny. He seemed to know what opponents and team-mates were going to do before they did, and he had the courage and intelligence to make tactical decisions in the heat of battle that most people are happy to sort out in the dressing-room inquest when it is too late.

He could lift and motivate players before vital matches with Churchillian-class rallying speeches, and he had a wit that was as sharp as a razorblade. It broke the hearts of those of us who knew him well to see him suffering from Alzheimer's disease later in his life.

I prefer my memories of him in his golden days when there was no better captain or more creative and authoritative wing-half in the game.

Danny was there on the pitch with me in my very first League match. It was August 1957 at White Hart Lane. I was making my debut for Chelsea against Tottenham, with Danny in the No 4 shirt. I got lucky and scored an equaliser after managing to sit several Tottenham players on their arses, including Danny. He put an arm around me as we came off at the final whistle, saying: "Well done, son. You have a big future in the game. Just remember to keep your feet on the ground, except when you're heading the ball." Typical Danny blarney.

A classic example of how he could turn things around came just before we played Atletico Madrid in Rotterdam in the 1963 European Cup-Winners' Cup final when we were bidding to become the first team to take a major European trophy back to Britain.

Our 'indestructible' Dave Mackay failed a fitness test shortly before the final, and this really shook manager Bill Nicholson, who like everybody else believed in the miracle that was Mackay. He was thoroughly miserable at the pre-match team talk and built Atletico Madrid up as the greatest team he had ever seen. The impression he had given us was that their defenders were as big as mountains and would crush any forward silly enough to go near them. He made their attack sound as if they had five forwards with the skill of di Stefano and the shooting power of Puskas. I knew that Bill Nick (one of the all-time great managers, of course) was trying to avoid any complacency among us, but he had overplayed it. He had frightened us to death!

As Bill Nick finished his dismal pre-match talk, Danny stood up and said as if he was a lawyer: 'If you don't mind, Boss, I'd like to say a word in our defence!' He then did a magnificent job repairing our shattered confidence. I wish I'd got what he said down on a tape-recorder because it was the most inspiring rallying speech I had ever heard and it would have served as a lesson to all managers and coaches how to lift and motivate a team before a vital match.

He told us to put ourselves in the place of the Atletico players and to imagine what they were thinking about us. We had the reputation of being one of the greatest club teams in the world and Danny, a master of the word game, convinced us that Atletico would be petrified. We won 5-1, and for once I was pleased to see Bill Nick proved hopelessly wrong with his analysis of a team.

This was all a million miles away from Danny's start in football, playing for Glentoran in his native Belfast while holding down a job as an apprentice electrician at Gallachers' cigarette factory ('I could see my life going up in smoke,' he said with typical humour).

He lied about his age to get into the RAF during the war and became a navigator. Perhaps this training helped him because in later years he definitely showed an exceptional navigational sense on the pitch.

Danny made a belated entry into the Football League when Barnsley paid Glentoran £6,000 for him in 1949, and he at last got the stage his skill deserved when he moved to Aston Villa for £15,000 in 1951. He told me he became disillusioned at Villa because 'they were living in the dark ages, training by lapping the pitch rather than being in the middle of the pitch with a football at their feet.'

It was his ten years at Tottenham that lifted him into the land of legend, captaining, encouraging and cajoling the first team of the Twentieth Century to win the League and FA Cup double. Three years earlier he suffered the anguish of hearing that his brother Jackie, Manchester United centre-half, had been so seriously injured in the Munich air crash that he never played again. They had been a formidable pair for Northern Ireland, and a bit of the sparkle went out of Danny after that family misfortune.

I joined Tottenham the season after the Double year following my Italian 'holiday', and we won the FA Cup by beating Burnley at Wembley in 1962 and then lifted the Cup Winners' Cup with that historic victory in Rotterdam.

A knee injury brought a premature end to Danny's career, and he switched to writing a column in the Sunday Express that was always readable and perceptive.

I thought he should have been groomed as successor to Bill Nick as manager at White Hart Lane, but when he did try his hand at management (with the Northern Ireland team and, briefly, with Chelsea) he suddenly seemed for the first time in his career to be lacking ideas and inspiration.

I had a chuckle to myself when Danny became the first person to tell Eamonn Andrews where to stuff his *This Is Your* Life book. 'The programme is an invasion of privacy and cheap entertainment for a voyeuristic public,' he said. I also happened to know that he was involved in a little romance on the side at the time, and did not want to risk this becoming public property.

He was always candid with his views and would never say things just for the sake of saying them. In 1967 CBS of America hired him as the colour commentator as soccer tried to get off the ground in the States. He was quickly sent packing when he continually told viewers the truth about the rubbish they were being served up by players who were either past their sell-by date or novices who could never dream of playing football Blanchflower- style.

Danny used to have us in fits with his off-the-cuff cracks, Irishisms that he used to offer tongue-in-cheek. A lot of it was blarney, but he would say: 'Blarney, yes, but never baloney.' Let's end with just a handful of his witty sayings in memory of not only one of the best but also the brightest of all footballers ...

'Our objective is to equalise before the other team score.'

'It's not winning that matters as much as wanting to win.'

'Everything in our favour was against us.'

'Have you noticed that ideas don't work unless you do?'

'If we don't know what we're going to do, how can the other side?'

'Football is so simple. While WE have the ball THEY can't score.'

'It's important to get our retaliation in first.'

'There's a move on to get bigger, wider goals. Surely it would be more economical to pick smaller, narrower goalkeepers.'

'I have come up with an idea how to slow the game down, because it has become far too helter-skelter. Let's play with square rather than round balls.'
'This idea of deciding drawn matches by penalties is so good that they should START the game with a penalty shoot-out and then play a match if the teams are tied.'

I was alongside Danny when a veteran Spurs director, who had been on the wrong end of Danny's cutting tongue, said: 'The trouble with you is that you think you know all the answers.'

Danny put an arm around his shoulder to soften the blow of his counter: 'Ah, God bless you, sir, but your problem is that you don't even know the questions.'

The team that Danny captained to the Double was as good as any club side ever seen in Britain, and I speak from having played against them and and it was the biggest honour of my footballing life when Bill Nick invited me to join them just a few months after their historic season. Danny greeted me like a long lost brother. "Jim" he said, "you are more than welcome. We should have been playing together years ago when spring was here, but let's enjoy the summer together." Yes, he was the poet of the team.

I confess to a tear in the eye as I think of him. The king of blarney and one helluva footballer, Danny Blanchflower. I close with what I thought was a fitting 'Oh Danny Boy' lament written by my old mate Norman Giller ...

Oh Danny Boy, the Spurs the Spurs are calling
From stand to stand and down the Shelf side
The summer's gone, but memories are flying
Of glory-glory days that have never died.
But come ye back when the pitch is in meadow
Or when The Lane's hushed and white with snow
'Tis we'll be there in sunshine and shadow
Oh Danny boy, oh Danny boy, we love you so.

First Division   White Hart Lane   Attendance: 47,605
TOTTENHAM 3, CARDIFF CITY 2

THIS was a scrambled victory for Tottenham against a Cardiff City side that played with spirit and high energy. Leading the First Division table by four points from Sheffield Wednesday, there was a tension in Tottenham's usually smooth play that suggested they were feeling the pressure of trying to maintain their unbeaten run.

Cardiff became only the second team of the season to score first against them when centre-forward Peter Donnelly escaped the attentions of Maurice Norman to beat the oncoming Bill Brown with a well-placed shot in the 20th minute. Terry Dyson celebrated as if he had won the FA Cup when he nodded in an equaliser from a Dave Mackay centre after 35 minutes. Just before half-time Terry Medwin thumped the ball into the net after a scintillating run by Les Allen, but Spurs were flattered by their 2-1 half-time lead.

Tottenham got their act together in the second-half and peppered the Cardiff goal with shots, but they lacked their usual accuracy. In the end Tottenham got a breathing-room two-goal lead when they were awarded a controversial penalty. The referee ruled that Steve Gammon had handled the ball when it was obvious that it was purely accidental. The Cardiff players were still complaining when Danny Blanchflower fired the ball high into the net from the spot.

Donnelly headed his and Cardiff's second goal from a Derek Tapscott centre in the 85th minute but Spurs held on for an untidy victory.

QUOTE – Bill Nicholson: ‘We have set standards for ourselves that mean we cannot be satisfied with this performance. We lacked our usual fluency in midfield, and our finishing was at times woeful. I admit we were fortunate with the penalty, but that's the way the game goes.’

TEAM AND SCORERS: Brown, Baker, Henry; Blanchflower, Norman, Mackay; Medwin, White, Smith, Allen, Dyson. Scorers: Medwin, Dyson, Blanchflower (pen).

First Division   White Hart Lane   Attendance 56,270
TOTTENHAM 5, FULHAM 1

GUY FAWKES Day, and it was Tottenham who provided the fireworks as they rocketed to a comfortable victory over Fulham. This stretched the Spurs lead over their nearest rivals Sheffield Wednesday to a commanding seven points, and there was a widespread view that even this early in the season the First Division championship was already destined for White Hart Lane for the first time since the Push and Run triumph of 1950-51.

Bill Nicholson took a calculated gamble in playing Cliff Jones, who had collected yet another niggling injury when taking part in a prestige inter-League match against Italy three days earlier. The flying winger came through the match in one piece, and scored with two typical diving headers that revealed both his class and his courage.

Les Allen also chipped in with two goals and John White got on the scoresheet against a Fulham side for whom Johnny Haynes was magnificent in midfield, but with team-mates who could not match his perfection. It could have been a much closer contest if bearded Jimmy Hill had accepted two golden chances created by Haynes, and if goalkeeper Tony Macedo had not gifted Tottenham two of their goals with elementary errors that had Haynes almost tearing his Brylcreemed hair out in frustration.

QUOTE – Johnny Haynes, Fulham and England skipper: ʻAs I was born in Edmonton I always had a soft spot for Tottenham, and Bill Nicholson made a couple of attempts to sign me, which would have been interesting. There is not a pro in the country who would not liked to have been part of that Double team. They played beautifully all season and thoroughly deserved their success. We were not in the same class. Very few teams were.ʼ

TEAM AND SCORERS: Brown, Baker, Henry; Blanchflower, Norman, Mackay; Jones, White, Smith, Allen, Dyson. Goalscorers: Allen (2), Jones (2), White.

Spurs hero 5: Maurice Norman

Art Turner 2010

Born Mulbarton, Norfolk, May 8 1934. Played 357 League matches for Spurs between 1955 and 1965, following one full season with his local club, Norwich City.

He was England's centre-half in 23 international matches and was shortlisted for World Cup duty in 1966 when his career was finished by a broken leg received in a Spurs friendly against the Hungarian national team.

At 6ft 1in and 13 stone, 'Big Monty' stood like an immovable mountain in the middle of the Spurs defence. He had joined Tottenham as a full-back, but it was his switch to centre-half that established him as one of the most reliable defenders in the League.

Mo made his international debut against Peru in 1962, and was England centre-half throughout the 1962 World Cup finals (Brazil eliminated them in the quarter-finals).

Big in build, big in heart and big in personality, with a lovely slow 'have-you-got-a-loight-boy' drawl, he helped make goalkeeper Bill Brown's job easier with his expert covering and support play. On those occasions when the usually dependable Brown made a mess of a cross you would usually find Mo thumping the ball away. But for tragically breaking a leg in a meaningless friendly match he would almost certainly have been England's centre-half in the 1966 World Cup finals and Jack Charlton might never have got his chance. On his retirement, Mo returned to his beloved Norfolk to concentrate on his gardening skills.

First Division   Hillsborough   Attendance 53,988
SHFFIELD WEDNESDAY 2, TOTTENHAM 1

THE record-breaking unbeaten run was finally torpedoed by a Sheffield Wednesday team lying in second place. It has been lost in the mists and myths of time that the previous season Tottenham had got off to a 12-match unbeaten start on their way to finishing third in the table. The run had ended at Hillsborough, so history was repeating itself.

Hillsborough has never been a happy hunting ground for Spurs, who had not won there since back in the 1937-38 season. Wednesday, protecting a 100 per cent unbeaten home record, snatched the lead through Billy Griffin just moments after Les Allen had what seemed a certain goal brilliantly saved by goalkeeper Roy McLaren.

Two minutes later, and with half-time beckoning, Dave Mackay took a quick free-kick and Maurice Norman galloped into the penalty area to head an equaliser.

Both teams played flat out in a see-sawing second-half, and after several near misses by the Spurs forwards the vital winning goal was collected by Wednesday's Johnny Fantham. He thumped the loose ball home after a comedy of errors in the packed Tottenham penalty area.

Dave Mackay played like a man possessed as he tore around the pitch trying to lift Tottenham into a comeback, but the Wednesday defence held out under a non-stop bombarment. It was rough and it was tough, but players from both sides went off with linked arms as a sporting finale to a memorable duel.

QUOTE – Danny Blanchflower: ꞌOnce the initial disappointment of losing had worn off we felt a huge rush of relief. Winning had become a burden! We sang and joked all the way back to London. Now we could concentrate on playing our natural game.ꞌ

TEAM AND SCORERS: Brown, Baker, Henry; Blanchflower, Norman, Mackay; Jones, White, Smith, Allen, Dyson. Goalscorer: Norman.

First Division   White Hart Lane   Attendance: 46,010
TOTTENHAM 6, BIRMINGHAM CITY 0

FREE from the pressure of HAVING to win, Spurs relaxed and started to play with their natural fluency and finesse. They purred to a 5-2 victory over Dinamo Tbilisi in a prestige friendly on the Monday and then, five days later, buried Birmingham under an avalanche of goals.

Les Allen was the man of the match, but his name does not appear on the scoresheet. The player better known for his goal scoring turned schemer and had a hand – or rather, a well-directed foot – in three of the goals.

The game was all over as a contest inside the first 17 minutes. John White ended a sweeping three-man movement with goal number one after just 130 seconds. Allen took three defenders out of contention six minutes later with a darting run before releasing the ball for Terry Dyson to make it 2-0.

The energetic Allen and Bobby Smith exchanged passes to create an opening for Cliff Jones to score in the 16th minute. Birmingham were rushed off their feet trying to hold back the flood of Tottenham attacks, and cracked in the last 20 minutes.

They conceded a headed goal by Jones, then a Smith penalty after Allen had been brought down. Dyson finished off the slaughter with a tap-in goal from close range after Birmingham's defence had been turned inside out by a series of beautifully composed raids.

The Spurs fans went home singing. They had witnessed 11 goals at The Lane in the last five days.

QUOTE – Bill Nicholson: 'We must guard against complacency. The season's only three months old, and I don't want to hear anybody talking about us having the title won. There is a long way to go.'

TEAM AND SCORERS: Brown, Baker, Henry; Blanchflower, Norman, Mackay; Jones, White, Smith, Allen, Dyson. Goalscorers: White, Dyson (2), Jones (2) Smith (pen)

First Division   The Hawthorns   Attendance 39,017

WEST BROMWICH ALBION 1, TOTTENHAM 3

TOTTENHAM continued their war on the Midlands clubs by beating a well-organised West Brom team at home, a victory that increased their runaway lead at the top of the First Division to an extraordinary nine points. And it was still November! Their nearest rivals, Everton and Sheffield Wednesday, both slipped up in what was becoming a despairing chase.

West Brom appealed with some justification that Bobby Smith was off-side as he accepted a pass from Cliff Jones before lashing the ball home to give Tottenham the lead in the 21st minute. The referee waved aside the Albion protests, and they were still grumbling when Smith added a second goal after a rapid four-man movement left their defence in a tormented tangle.

The ball travelled the length of the Hawthorns pitch on a conveyor belt of passes from Tottenham's goalmouth for goal number three, neatly tucked away by Les Allen from close range.

Right-back Don Howe, England's No 2 and later a coach and manager of note, pulled a goal back for West Brom before half-time, but hard as they tried they could not pierce the Tottenham defence in a slog of a second-half.

QUOTE – Don Howe: ⁶The Spurs team of 1960-61 was one of the best club combinations of all time. We worked hard on tactical plans to stifle their magnificent midfield trio, from whom so many of their attacks flowed. But they were so flexiblke that they were able to change the emphasis so that suddenly the main threat was coming down the wings. We were pushed and pulled all over the place. They were a joy to watch, provided you were not playing against them! ⁹

TEAM AND SCORERS: Brown, Baker, Henry; Blanchflower, Norman, Mackay; Jones, White, Smith, Allen, Dyson. Goalscorers: Smith (2), Allen.

Dave Mackay, the heart of Tottenham's Double masters

An appreciation of *DAVE MACKAY*
By Jimmy Greaves

JIMMY GREAVES rates Dave Mackay the greatest all-round footballer ever to wear a Spurs shirt. Here, exclusively for our book and No 6 in the Spurs Heroes Profile series, he gives a personal assessment of the Great Scot:

Born Edinburgh November 14, 1934
Career span: 1953-72
Clubs: Hearts 1953-59 (135 games, 25 goals), Tottenham 1959-68 (268 League games, 42 goals), Derby County 1968-71 (122 League games, 5 goals), Swindon 1971-72 (26 League games, 1 goal)
Club honours: 1 Scottish League title and 1 Scottish FA Cup with Hearts; 1 League title, 3 FA Cups and 1 European Cup Winners' Cup with Tottenham (a medal was awarded even though he missed the final through injury), Second Division title with Derby County.
Scotland: 22 caps (4 goals)
Footballer of the Year (1969, shared with Man City's Tony Book)

WHILE Danny Blanchflower was the silky smooth poet of the outstanding Tottenham team of the 'sixties, Dave Mackay was the swashbuckling pirate; Danny the brains, Dave the heart. He matched Blanchflower's passing and surpassed his passion. Never throughout my career did I play with a more inspirational team-mate. One look at his clenched fist, and I felt I had been transported to the battlefield of Bannockburn. You could almost hear the bagpies skirling when the magnificent Mackay was in full cry.

Waxing lyrical? Yes, well that is the effect the marvellous memories of Dave Mackay have on me. You know when you were a kid in the playground and used to pick teams at random? Dave would always have been my first choice because he had a bit of everything. There was the skilful left foot, the ability to drill a 40-yard pass with accuracy, the never-give-up competitive spirit, and a tackle that was like the scythe of a claymore.

For all the baubles he won in the game, both as a player and manager, his greatest victory was over adversity. He twice made comebacks after breaking a leg. Not for nothing was he known as the 'Miracle Man' of football.

If somebody put a gun to my head and insisted that I name the greatest player in that marvellous 'Super Spurs' side it would have to be Dave Mackay. He had just about everything in his arsenal (oops, poor choice of word ... let's say in his locker). He had power, skill, drive, stamina and showed the sort of heroism that would have won medals in wartime.

Nobody from my generation will ever forget that unforgettable photograph snapped by legendary *Daily Mirror* photographer Monte Fresco of Dave holding Leeds United hard man Billy Bremner by the shirt collar and frightening the shite out of him with a brandished fist. This was after Wild Billy had been foolish enough to try to challenge him in a tackling contest at White Hart Lane. It was the Master putting the apprentice in his place.

'Billy was a pal of mine,' said Dave. 'But like a lot of that Leeds team he could be a nasty bugger on the pitch, and he went into a tackle against me that could have led to me breaking my leg again. I just let him know what I thought of him and warned what would happen if he tried it again. That picture served to haunt me because it's the one people always ask me to sign, and it gives the impression that I was a bully of a player. I like to think I was fair. Firm but fair. Okay, very firm, but fair.'

Dave had infectious enthusiasm, and I often offered up a silent prayer that he was with me and not against me. I have shuddered at some of his tackles on rival players, and he used to go in just as hard after those two broken leg set-backs. The first time he broke his leg, the right one, it enraged everybody in the Tottenham team. Man United skipper Noel Cantwell went roaring into a 50-50 tackle with no intention of playing the ball, and his boot thudded into Dave's shin. This was in a European Cup-Winners' Cup tie at Old Trafford, and the crack of breaking bone could be heard around the ground. Dave was understandably bitter about that, and from then on he always called Cantwell 'Cant', and making it sound as close as possible to the c*** word. They made it up after both had retired, but for the rest of his playing career he was planning a revenge hit on 'Cant.'

I am doing him an injustice in presenting Dave as all power and passion, and playing on the edge of violence. His tacking was always fair, and he was never ever sent off. Bill Nicholson would not have entertained or encouraged any play that was dirty or

Artist Art Turner's impression of the moment that Dave Mackay put Leeds United's Billy Bremner in his place at White Hart Lane on the first day of the 1966-67 season.

cynical. Dave had delicate skills to go with his natural strength. Bobby Moore is one of the few defenders I can think of who could rival him for ball control in a tight situation. The swaggering Scot was the king of the first-time pass, drilling the ball through to a team-mate as accurately and as casually as if in a training stint; this despite being under pressure from an opponent.

Dave took over from Danny as Spurs captain, and I can safely say that I played under the two greatest club skippers that ever carried a ball on to the pitch.

He didn't suffer fools off the pitch, and could be blunt to the point of rudeness with anybody who poked their nose in where he didn't think it belonged. Football writers either became very close friends with him (particularly if they got in the first round), or were barred enemies. He could be just as lacking in tolerance with any team-mates who stepped out of line, and I recall him putting Terry Venables swiftly in his place when he was a bit too cocky for Dave's taste on his arrival at Tottenham from Chelsea.

He liked to be the top man in training as well as in match play, and I recall a trick he had that made us all respectful of his ability. He would continually volley the ball against the wall from twelve yards in our indoor gymnasium at White Hart Lane. It sounds easy, but just try it. Remember, it has to be a succession of shots without the ball touching the ground.

Another fond memory I have is of following Dave as he led us out on to the pitch. As he crossed the white line he would go through his pre-match ritual of kicking the ball high in the air and then catching it on his instep. It was just a little reminder to the opposition players and fans that he could play a bit.

Here's a little statistic that I offer to help add to the legend of Mackay: He played in more than forty cup finals at all levels during his career, and was never once on the losing side! That illustrates what I mean about his competitive spirit. He just hated to lose, and would sink into a depression if ever we lost a game, particularly at home at White Hart Lane. Whether he was playing snooker, darts, tiddlywinks or cards, he would pour every ounce of his concentration into trying to win.

It's amazing now to think that Bill Nicholson bought him from Hearts for £32,000 more by accident than design. He had been chasing Mel Charles at Swansea, and only switched to Mackay after losing out to Arsenal in the race to sign the Welsh giant.

People always got a surprise when they met Dave for the first time away from the football field. The impression given was that he was some sort of colossus, a picture in the mind helped by the fact that he had a barrel chest that he always stuck out with pride when leading his troops into battle.

Yet he stood a sliver under 5ft 8in (despite what the record books might say) and weighed around twelve stone. But he made his mark on every game with such fire and fury that there were times when he frightened me to death – and I was on his side.

Dave will always carry two scars hidden away for private moments of grief. He was in the Scottish schoolboys team beaten 8-2 at the old Wembley by an England team captained by 15-year-old Johnny Haynes.

Nine years later he was in the Scotland team decimated 9-3 at Wembley by an England team captained by 24-year-old Johnny Haynes. If you value your life, you daren't mention those two results in Dave's hearing. Like I say, he was not the best of losers and those two defeats will have cost him lots of sleep.

The 9-3 defeat came in the season that Spurs won the League and FA Cup double, one of the great achievements of the 20th Century. I played against that wonderful team while I was wearing a Chelsea shirt, and it was unanimously agreed among the Stamford Bridge squad that they were as good as any championship side any of us had ever seen. It was my pleasure and privilege to join them the following season for what were the best years of my footballing life.

The few times Dave could bring himself to mention that 9-3 destruction in my hearing he would say, "It could have been 9-3 to us if we had swapped goalkeepers." And it has to be admitted that at least three of our goals were down to the errors of poor Frank Haffey, who later emigrated to New Zealand to get away from being sniggered in the back. "What's the time?" they used to ask? "Nine past Haffey."

I remember when Dave was persuaded to join Derby County at the back end of his career. Brian Clough, who knew better than anybody that he had a passion for playing that money could not buy, locked him in an office at White Hart Lane and brow beat him until he agreed to sign a contract.

Later, Dave was close to tears when he told me he did not really want to go to Derby because his heart was still at Tottenham.

He hated the thought of leaving all his mates – he was the king of our drinking school at the White Hart – and he had a lucrative club-tie manufacturing company that he ran with his business partner Jimmy Burton.

Dave was not only a great warrior but something of a worrier too, and he went through agonies over his decision to finally lay down his shield at Spurs and follow the then relatively inexperienced manager Clough on the road to what he considered the football outpost of Derby.

He thought Bill Nicholson should have given him another two seasons at Spurs, but Bill knew the Mackay engine was running out and did not feel he could sustain his midfield-marauding style. And he knew that waiting in the wings he had the bright young, full-of-energy Steve Perryman to fill his boots.

What Bill Nick didn't realise was that Cloughie had no intention of playing Dave in his old midfield motivating role. With a tactical move that showed Cloughie's genius as a manager, he switched Dave to the heart of the Derby defence. Here he was able to stroll rather than sprint alongside a promising young centre-half called Roy McFarland, and he could conserve energy while others did the running, the chasing and the feuding. It was a master stroke by Clough, and in the sunset of his career Dave led Derby to the Second Division championship.

He was at last elected Footballer of the Year in 1969, yet it came with the slight of having to share it with Manchester City skipper Tony Book. Dave Mackay was on his own.

Dave could not get football out of his bones, and in an eventful managing career he steered Derby to the First Division championship in 1974-75 after taking over in controversial circumstances from his former boss Brian Clough. He also managed Swindon Town, Nottingham Forest, Walsall, Doncaster Rovers and Birmingham City, and had a successful coaching career in the Middle East.

Whenever I see Dave as the pair of us go into the autumn of our years we always give each other a warm hug like the old friends that we are, and I regale anybody within earshot that he was one of the all-time greats. The Scottish selectors rewarded him with only twenty-two caps back in the days when they tended to sneer at exiles. Had he been born an Englishman, he would have followed England skipper Billy Wright into the 100-cap category.

But had he been born on our side of the border, he might have lacked the passion of the Real Mackay.

First Division   White Hart Lane   Attendance 58,737
TOTTENHAM 4, BURNLEY 4

DEFENDING League champions Burnley were determined not to let their crown go without a fight, and they produced a proud, passionate performance in this eight-goal classic on a soaking-wet White Hart Lane pitch. Driven from midfield by Jimmy McIlroy – Danny Blachflower's Northern Ireland team-mate and best friend – the Lancastrians might easily have been two goals clear in the opening minutes with kinder luck and better finishing.

A three-goal burst in a four-minute spell by Tottenham would have killed off most teams. Maurice Norman sparked the quick-fire goal storm in the 18th minute with a firm header from a corner, followed by Cliff Jones finding the net twice in just over a minute as he tortured the usually sound Burnley defence. It all seemed just a question of how many goals could Tottenham score when Dave Mackay made it 4-0 in the 36th minute to send the champions reeling on the mudheap of a pitch.

England winger John Connelly pulled one back before half-time, yet few people gave Burnley a hope of getting back into the game. But they had not won the championship without showing great character to go with their class, and rare mistakes by, first Ron Henry, and then Norman let Jimmy Robson and Ray Pointer in for unexpected goals.

Spurs responded with an all-out assault on the Burnley goal, but left themselves open for a counter attack and it was John Connelly who finished the scoring spree after exchanging passes with Robson in the 78th minute. Both teams were given a standing ovation at the final whistle.

QUOTE – Jimmy McIlroy: ❛I wouldn't want Danny Blanchflower to know I said this, but we have just stolen a point from the next champions. Nobody is going to stop them taking our title.❜

TEAM AND SCORERS: Brown, Baker, Henry; Blanchflower, Norman, Mackay; Jones, White, Smith, Allen, Dyson. Goalscorers: Norman, Jones (2), Mackay.

First Division   Deepdale   Attendance: 21,657
PRESTON 0, TOTTENHAM 1

APPALLING December weather kept the Deepdale attendance down to under 22,000 spectators, the lowest crowd that Spurs attracted all season. There was a mood of doom and gloom at once-Proud Preston, who were 18th in the table and struggling against the threat of relegation. The downbeat atmosphere seemed to creep into Tottenham's usual poise and purpose, and they struggled to gain control.

Manager Bill Nicholson was forced to make a rare team change when Bobby Smith reported that he was feeling unwell, and the willing youngster Frank Saul was summoned to once again fill the No 9 shirt.

Without their top scorer, Tottenham lacked their usual finishing punch and the Three Musketeers in midfield – Danny Blanchflower, John White and Dave Mackay – were not functioning with the dynamic drive that had made them the talk of football.

The treacherous pitch surface made every step a challenge, but the Tottenham defence was rarely under serious threat from a Preston team lacking in ideas and inspiration. How they were missing the recently retired Tom Finney.

A far from satisfactory victory was finally clinched when Maurice Norman made his usual run upfield for a corner. He headed the ball down and John White was first to react in a crowded goalmouth and he squeezed the ball into the net to put Tottenham on the way to their first 1-0 victory of the season.

QUOTE – Bill Nicholson: *'We can consider ourselves fortunate to have come away with both points. The conditions were not condusive to our style of football, but we have to accept that this was a very untidy performance. We cannot afford to rest on our laurels.'*

TEAM AND SCORERS: Brown, Baker, Henry; Blanchflower, Norman, Mackay; Jones, White, Saul, Allen, Dyson. Goalscorers: White.

First Division   Goodison Park   Attendance 61,052
EVERTON 1, TOTTENHAM 3

NOT too many of the Spurs supporters who made the long trek to Goodison for the match against second-placed Everton could tell you too much in detail about an outstanding win. A curtain of fog dropped on Merseyside and visibility was seriously affected. Scottish schemer Bobby Collins, small but dynamic, was challenging Blanchflower and White for midfield supremacy, and he had the better of the early exchanges. He set up three chances in the opening minutes that were all squandered by his team-mates.

The game started to swing Tottenham's way when Dave Mackay switched from the left to the right side of midfield to stifle the influence of Collins. This released Blanchflower to play his natural attacking game and he was the instigator of two goals in four minutes, first putting Cliff Jones clear to create a goal for John White and then combining with White and Terry Dyson to open the way for Dyson to make it 2-0.

Everton could not believe that they were trailing by two goals in a match they had been monopolising, and they opened the second-half as they had the first, with a barrage of attacks. At the peak of their pressure Alex 'The Golden Vision' Young and flying Irish winger Billy Bingham set up Frank Wignall for a goal from close range.

The fog was almost heavy enough to cause an abandonment when Dave Mackay settled where the points were going with a spectacular 35 yard left-foot drive into the top corner of the net. Few people in the ground saw it, including Everton goalkeeper Albert Dunlop.

QUOTE – Everton manager John Carey: ⁶You just cannot afford not to take your chances against an outstanding team like Tottenham. We should have been two goals clear, and then they punished us.⁹

TEAM AND SCORERS: Brown, Baker, Henry; Blanchflower, Norman, Mackay; Jones, White, Smith, Allen, Dyson. Goalscorers: White, Dyson, Mackay.

Art Turner 2010

Born Swansea February 7 1935. Scored 135 goals in 318 League matches for Spurs after joining them from Swansea for £35,000 in February 1958. He won a then record 59 Welsh international caps and had the final shots of his career with Fulham, for whom he signed in 1968 after collecting a string of honours with Spurs.

Through much of his career and after he retired, he had an interest in a butcher-shop business in the days when players had to supplement their income from the game.

Cliff stood 5ft 7in tall, weighed just over 10 stone, and moved like a whippet along either wing for Spurs and Wales. Football was in his blood. He was the son of pre-war Welsh international Ivor Jones, and the nephew of former Arsenal and Wales inside-forward Bryn, and the brother of long-serving League professional Bryn Jnr. His cousin, Ken Jones, was an ex-pro who became one of the country's leading sports columnists.

At his peak, Cliff was without doubt one of the world's greatest wingers. He used to run with the pace and determination of a Welsh wing three-quarter. Brave to the point of madness in the penalty area, he used to rise like a salmon at the far post to head spectacular goals. Cliff was happiest on the left wing, but agreed to spend much of the Double season on the right to allow for the left-footed Terry Dyson to come in at outside-left. When you talk about great wingers like Matthews, Finney and Best you can mention Cliff Jones in the same breath.

First Division   White Hart Lane   Attendance 65,930
TOTTENHAM 2, WEST HAM UNITED 0

CHRSTMAS EVE and Boxing Day home and away matches against West Ham gave Spurs the chance to cement their lead at the top of the table, which had now stretched to an overwhelming ten points. The Hammers, their attack led by Tottenham old boy Dave Dunmore, battled bravely at The Lane but went down to two headed goals – the first by John White in the 28th minute and the second in the closing moments of the game by Terry Dyson. The 65,930 crowd was the biggest of the season.

Remarkably, the goals from White and Dyson meant that every Spurs forward had reached double figures in the League with the season not even halfway through. The scoring tally was: Bobby Smith (18 goals), Les Allen (12), Cliff Jones, John White and Terry Dyson ten goals each.

In all, Tottenham had amassed 73 goals. Their gung-ho attacking methods came at the price of something of a leaking defence – with 22 goals conceded. Danny Blanchflower gave little heed to defensive duties, which meant that Peter Baker had to work hard to cover for him. But proof that Danny's attacking attitude was a key factor is that many of the goals scored had a pass from Danny stitched into the build-up.

West Ham, in a transitional period before the emergence of youngsters Geoff Hurst and Martin Peters to join Bobby Moore, played some neat, thoughtfull football, but without causing goalkeeper Bill Brown too many problems. There was less pressure on the Hammers when Cliff Jones limped out of the game on the hour with damaged ligaments, this of course in the pre-substitute days.

QUOTE – Bill Nicholson: ‘Considering we had Cliff Jones injured inside the first minute of the second-half and Bill Brown handicapped by a swollen ankle, we have to feel satisfied with our performance.’

TEAM AND SCORERS: Brown, Baker, Henry; Blanchflower, Norman, Mackay; Jones, White, Smith, Allen, Dyson. Goalscorers: White, Dyson.

First Division   Upton Park   Attendance: 34,351
WEST HAM UNITED 0, TOTTENHAM 3

PERHAPS West Ham had more Christmas pudding than the Tottenham players; whatever it was, they were almost completely outplayed in the return match at Upton Park. The final scoreline flattered the Hammers, who had to work their socks off to avoid being humiliated.

For the first time in the season, manager Bill Nicholson was forced to make two changes: John Hollowbread taking over in goal from Bill Brown, and Terry Medwin coming in for Cliff Jones.

Centre-half Ken Brown conceded West Ham's first goal, turning the ball into his own net as he tried to divert a Les Allen shot. Allen did not need any help with the second goal, making it 2-0 after controlling a paralysing pass from Dave Mackay. Allen and Brown had grown up together in Bolland Road, Dagenham. but their friendship was put on hold for 90 minutes.

West Ham, with Welsh international Phil Woosnam pulling the strings in midfield, made a bright start to the second-half, and 19-year-old Bobby Moore was ready to celebrate a rare goal when Hollowbread leapt high to pluck the net-bound shot out of the air.

The match-clinching third goal was a thing of beauty that had even West Ham fans applauding in appreciation. The ball travelled on a magic carpet of 13 ground passes before John White finished the magnificent move with an angled shot that gave goalkeeper Brian Rhodes no chance.

Bookmakers were now refusing to take bets on Tottenham winning the League championship. Wolves were back in second place but ten points adrift of the unstoppable Lilywhites.

QUOTE – Danny Blanchflower: ❛Bill Nicholson is never an easy man to please, but even he had to admit that at times in this match against West Ham we touched Everest-peaks of perfection.❜

TEAM AND SCORERS: Hollowbread, Baker, Henry; Blanchflower, Norman, Mackay; Medwin, White, Smith, Allen, Dyson. Scorers: Brown (own goal), White, Allen.

First Division   White Hart Lane   Attendance 48,742
TOTTENHAM 5, BLACKBURN ROVERS 2

TOTTENHAM rang out the old year with a resounding victory over Blackburn Rovers on an almost spring-like day at The Lane. Even without Spurs braveheart Dave Mackay, Tottenham bossed the midfield after England winger Bryan Douglas fired Rovers into a 1-0 lead completely against the run of play in the 14th minute.

Bobby Smith chested an equaliser from a Terry Dyson cross in the 37th minute, and then – with Tony Marchi fitting comfortably into the Mackay shirt – Tottenham took command.

They ripped Blackburn apart with a series of rapid raids in the second-half, and collected four goals in a 20-minute burst of brilliance. Les Allen volleyed the ball into the Blackburn net in the 57th minute, and two minutes later skipper Blanchflower nonchantly swept the ball home after running on to a neat back-heel from Bobby Smith. Allen and Smith made it 5-1 before Peter Dobing replied with a late goal for shell-shocked Rovers.

Much to the undisguised annoyance of Bill Nicholson, all the talk as 1960 gave way to 1961 was of whether Spurs could go on to win the elusive double of League championship and FA Cup. They came into the New Year with a ten point lead over Wolves, and so the first leg of the Double – the League title – was almost certainly already wrapped up.

QUOTE – Danny Blanchflower: ‘I had stopped talking about the possibility of the elusive Double because I knew it irritated Bill Nicholson, but now with the FA Cup challenge around the corner it was the hottest of all topics with the media. It was a bit unsettling to find the so-called experts predicting that there was not a team in the country that could stop us. Yet it was supposed to be the Impossible Dream.’

TEAM AND SCORERS: Brown, Baker, Henry; Blanchflower, Norman, Marchi; Jones, White, Smith, Allen, Dyson. Goalscorers: Smith (2), Allen (2), Blanchflower.

FA CUP, Third Round

January 7 1961   White Hart Lane   Attendance 54,969
TOTTENHAM 3, CHARLTON ATHLETIC 2

THE FA Cup adventure started with a home third round tie against Charlton Athletic as a revolution loomed on the football horizon. For all their success in this 1960-61 season, the Tottenham players were being paid the £20 maximum wage – earning exactly the same as the footballers at Accrington Stanley down in the Fourth Division. PFA chairman Jimmy Hill announced that the players had agreed, controversially, on a nationwide footballers' strike on January 21.

Charlton, dreaming of Wembley from a mid-table position in the Second Division, gave an excellent account of themselves after going two goals down inside the first 30 minutes. The goals were like carbon copies, Danny Blanchflower slicing the defence apart with measured passes that Les Allen swept into the Charlton net.

Skipper Stuart Leary, Charlton's South African-born Kent cricketer, pulled a goal back in the 33rd minute, but Terry Dyson quickly restored the two-goal lead and once again it was a pass from the imperious Blanchflower that created the chance.

The second-half was barely a minute old when Sam Lawrie snatched a goal for Charlton that brought sudden tension to a game Tottenham had been monopolising with ease. Just as it seemed inevitable that Charlton would force an equaliser and earn a replay, it was that man Blanchflower who took command in midfield and slowed the frantic pace of the game, which took the sting out of the Charlton comeback.

QUOTE – Dave Mackay: ⁶Charlton showed just why we must not take any match for granted. People think it's so easy for us because of our record this season, but there is no such thing as an easy game. We must not lose our concentration and determination.⁹

TEAM AND SCORERS: Brown, Baker, Henry; Blanchflower, Norman, Mackay; Jones, White, Smith, Allen, Dyson. Goalscorers: Allen (2), Dyson.

First Division   Old Trafford   Attendance 65,535
MANCHESTER UNITED 2, TOTTENHAM 0

TO a backdrop of the news that the Football League hierarchy had capitulated and agreed to the kicking out of the maximum wage, the Manchester United players celebrated by handing Tottenham their second defeat of the season. Spurs would not seek to make excuses as, without argument, the better side won on the day, but they lacked their usual rhythm because of injury-forced team changes. For the first time, they failed to find the back of the net.

Peter Baker, Cliff Jones and Terry Medwin were all sidelined for a game switched to the Monday evening after fog caused a postponement on the Saturday. Welshman Ken Barton came in for his League debut at right-back, and John Smith filled in for Terry Medwin. Smith had joined Spurs from West Ham, with Dave Dunmore moving as part of the deal. The idea was that he would eventually replace the ageing Danny Blanchflower, but Danny Boy had no intention of stepping down!

It was 18-year-old Nobby Stiles who gave United the lead in the 13th minute, but you would have got good odds on Tottenham coming back into the match when United goalkeeper Harry Gregg went off with a damaged shoulder a minute before half-time. Centre-forward Alex Dawson took over in goal and pulled off a series of unlikely saves – applauded by Gregg, who had come back on the pitch heavily strapped and playing a nuisance role in attack. It was Gregg's cheeky back heel that set up a victory-clinchng goal for Mark Pearson in the 74th minute.

QUOTE – Harry Gregg: ⁶I have always told the other players that playing up front is easy compared with keeping goal. I thoroughly enjoyed myself, and loved playing a part in the crucial second goal. But let's not take anything away from Spurs. They are exceptional.⁹

TEAM AND SCORERS: Brown, Barton, Henry; Blanchflower, Norman, Mackay; J. Smith, White, R. Smith, Allen, Dyson.

Born Musselburgh, Lothian, April 28 1937. Scored 40 goals in 183 League games for Spurs after signing from Falkirk in 1959 for £20,000. He was capped 22 times by Scotland and was an 'ever present' for Spurs during the Double season.

In his youth he had been turned down by both Glasgow Rangers and Middlesbrough as being too small, but he quickly showed that his frail appearance was misleading.

Art Turner
2010

Bill Nicholson bought him on the advice of both Dave Mackay and Danny Blanchflower, who had seen him in action for Scotland. He took time to settle to the pace of League football, but once attuned became one of the finest schemers in the game.

He was so aptly nicknamed 'The Ghost of White Hart Lane.' It was his ability off the ball that made him such a phenomenal player. He would pop up from out of nowhere just when he was needed most to make a pass or collect the ball. Like Danny Blanchflower, he had the gift of being able to give the exact weight to a pass, so that the ball would arrive where and when it was needed. John had the energy to run all day and could cut a defence in half with just one cunningly placed ball.

The year after helping Spurs capture the European Cup-Winners' Cup in 1963 he was struck down and killed by a bolt of lightning while sheltering under a tree during a solo round of golf.

First Division   White Hart Lane   Attendance 65,251
TOTTENHAM 4, ARSENAL 2

BEST moment of the season so far for true-blue Tottenham fans as they completed the double over their sworn enemies from Highbury via Woolwich. There was an early fright for Spurs when Scottish international right-half Tommy Docherty created the opening for Jackie Henderson to fire Arsenal into the lead, but Les Allen quickly cancelled it out from a quality pass by John White.

Terry Neill, red-blooded 18-year-old Irish defender, made a rash tackle on Terry Dyson and his countryman Danny Blanchflower coolly slotted home the penalty to make it 2-1. Tottenham's third goal deserved to be captured in oils as Dave Mackay almost arrogantly exchanged passes with Peter Baker before releasing the ball to Cliff Jones. He accelerated deep into Arsenal territory and then centred for Bobby Smith to tap in from close range. Arsenal's players looked stunned as they went in at half-time trailing 3-1 in a match in which they had been giving as good as they got.

The second-half got off to a dramatic start with two goals in as many minutes. Les Allen collected his second goal after a John White shot had been blocked, and Joe Harvey replied for Arsenal during a rare moment of indecision at the heart of the Tottenham defence.

Battle-hardened Tommy Docherty tried desperately to drive Arsenal back into the match, but he finally had to concede defeat in a midfield melting pot where his countrymen Mackay and White reigned supreme.

QUOTE – Tommy Docherty: ❛I always held up that Spurs team of 1960-61 as an example of how football should be played. Billy Nicholson was an outstanding manager and coach, and kept things nice and simple. There have been few midfield trios in club football to match Blanchflower, White and Mackay. They were fantastic.❜

TEAM AND SCORERS: Brown, Baker, Henry; Blanchflower, Norman, Mackay; Jones, White, Smith, Allen, Dyson. Goalscorers: Allen (2), Blanchflower (pen), Smith.

*T*HIS *is how the top football writers and columnists were reporting on the Tottenham march towards the Double in the days when Fleet Street newspapers were selling like hot bagels in Tel Aviv ...*

GEOFFREY GREEN, *The Times*: 'The Glasgow Orpheus Choir, the Duke Ellington Orchestra, the Royal Ballet Company ... Tottenham Hotspur, all perfect collectivism. I am moved to put the Spurs side in this exalted company because they have a rhythm about them that could be set to music. If any team is equipped to capture the elusive League Championship and FA Cup it is this side put together with care and consideration by manager Bill Nicholson ...'

DESMOND HACKETT, *Daily Express*: 'Danny Blanchflower confided in me some six months ago that this would be the season that Tottenham Hotspur did the 'impossible' by becoming the first team this 61 year old century to win not only the League Championship but also the FA Cup. Here we are in January, and I for one believe that the pipes, the pipes are calling that Danny Boy is going to be proved right ...'

PETER LORENZO, *Daily Herald*: 'Bill Nicholson is a blunt man who refuses to get caught up in speculation about the chances of Tottenham Hotspur breaking the Double jinx. "I don't go in for fairytales," he told me. "I work on fact, and I will admit the League title is now within our sights, but the FA Cup is a different proposition altogether. It can end in a moment during a cold, windy afternoon somewhere unexpected. To win the League you need good planning and consistency. To win the FA Cup you need luck." Well I for one believe the Double is on its way to White Hart Lane ... given a little luck.'

IAN WOOLDRIDGE, *News Chronicle*: 'It was impossible they said to conquer Mount Everest. "Wrong," said Edmund Hillary in 1953. It was impossible they said to break the four-minute mile barrier. "Wrong," said Roger Bannister in 1954. It is impossible they are saying to win the League Championship trophy and the FA Cup in the same season. "Wrong," said Danny Blanchflower last August, and this elegant and eloquent master of football is now putting forward a compelling argument with his feet that the Double CAN and WILL be done ... '

FRANK McGHEE, *Daily Mirror:* 'There have been Manchester United teams of the 1940s and 1950s – in particular the Busby Babes – and Wolves sides of recent memory who can lay claim to being the finest club teams since the war. Well stand by to accept that they are all going to be eclipsed by this Tottenham side that I have, with justification, labelled Super Spurs. There is not a weakness in this team that Bill Nicholson built, and I will be astonished if they do not become the first team this 20th Century to win both the League title and the FA Cup ... '

ALAN HOBY, *Sunday Express*: 'We are watching the progress of a Tottenham team that should be relished and cherished like vintage wine. As a veteran of many a press box and many a match, you know there is something special happening when football journalists start reaching for new descriptive phrases and polishing adjectives that have not been used since the relief of Mafeking. The current Spurs team is lighting up the face of soccer and making not only Tottenham supporters but neutrals smile with football that is beautiful to witness. Here we are in mid-winter with the League championship virtually already in the Spurs trophy cabinet, and bookmakers petrified to take bets on the Double ... '

FA CUP, Fourth Round

January 28   White Hart Lane   Attendance: 63,721
TOTTENHAM 5, CREWE ALEXANDRA 1

THERE was amusement and amazement mixed with a little apprehension when Tottenham were drawn against Crewe Alexandra for a fourth round FA Cup tie at White Hart Lane. It is part of Tottenham folklore how they played Crewe at the same stage of the tournament the previous season. They were held to a draw at Crewe and then won the replay by a club record 13-2. Both Bill Nicholson and his captain Danny Blanchflower spent the week leading up to the 1961 tie preaching against the dangers of complacency.

Just for the record, this was the team and the goal scorers in that 1960 replay: Brown, Hills, Henry, Blanchflower, Norman, Mackay, White, Harmer, Smith, Allen, Jones. The score was 6-1 inside the first 30 minutes and 10-1 at half-time. Les Allen scored five goals, Bobby Smith four, Cliff Jones a hat-trick and tiny Tommy Harmer's rare long-range shot completed the rout.

There could easily have been double figures again in the 1961 tie but for a string of brilliant saves by Crewe goalkeeper Brian Williamson. The game was all over as a contest by half-time, following goals by Terry Dyson, Bobby Smith and Dave Mackay to one goal from Terry Tighe for a gallant but outclassed Crewe side.

Thanks mainly to the at times miraculous work of Williamson, Tottenham were confined to just two more goals in the second-half from Cliff Jones and Les Allen.

QUOTE – Bobby Smith: ‘All the talk after the comfortable win against Crewe was about the Double. It put us under enormous pressure because history was against us. But we were quietly confident that we could do it.’

TEAM AND SCORERS: Brown, Baker, Henry; Blanchflower, Norman, Mackay; Jones, White, Smith, Allen, Dyson. Goalscorers: Dyson, Smith, Mackay, Jones, Allen.

First Division   White Hart Lane   Attendance 53,627
TOTTENHAM 2, LEICESTER CITY 3

IT was nearly six months coming, but for the first time in this glorious season Tottenham tasted defeat at White Hart Lane. The unlikely winners were a Leicester City team who had been consistent only in their inconsistency, and much to manager Bill Nicholson's anger Spurs were caught in the clutches of complacency.

Even the usually fervent Tottenham fans seemed to lack their customary commitment. The decibel count was well down as Leicester sneaked into a surprise 29th minute lead, Ken Leek beating Bill Brown with a thumping drive.

The goal acted as an alarm call to Spurs, and Les Allen ran on to a Cliff Jones pass five minutes later to stroke the ball past the oncoming Gordon Banks. Just as the Spurs fans were thinking normal service had been resumed, Leicester regained the lead in the 38th minute when Leek headed the ball against the bar and bundled the rebound into the net.

Bill Nick gave his players a half-time rollocking and they came out for the second-half with clear intent to regain control of the game. Their equalizer in the opening minutes was courtesy of a Blanchflower penalty after Bobby Smith was adjudged to have been fouled.

Suddenly there was an element of ill will in the game, and Dave Mackay was booked following an angry clash with Len Chalmers. Tottenham had lost their composure … and they lost the match when Maurice Norman dithered over a clearance. Jimmy Walsh stole the ball from him and gleefully poked it past Bill Brown for a shock 67th minute winner.

QUOTE – Danny Blanchflower: ❛This is the wake up call we need. Winning has become too easy a habit. We have been reminded that you have to earn victory.❜

TEAM AND SCORERS: Brown, Baker, Henry; Blanchflower, Norman, Mackay; Jones, White, Smith, Allen, Dyson. Goalscorers: Allen, Blanchflower (pen).

First Division   Villa Park   Attendance 50,786
ASTON VILLA 1, TOTTENHAM 2

BY one of those freak coincidences often thrown up by the fixture fates, Spurs travelled to play Aston Villa in the League a week before having to play them again in the fifth round of the FA Cup. Tottenham's confidence had been shaken by the Leicester City defeat, and they played with more caution than usual in a tense first-half. Villa had clearly decided that Danny Blanchflower was the man who made Spurs tick, and they double parked defenders on him in a bid to stifle his input.

Tottenham had a lucky escape late in a goalless first-half when Ron Henry clearly handled the ball in the goalmouth, but the referee was unsighted and waved play on as he ignored the animated penalty appeals of the Villa players.

Half-time pies were still being digested when Bobby Smith escaped the suffocating company of Villa defender Jimmy Dugdale to head Tottenham into the lead, answering manager Bill Nicholson's call for a quick strike..

Villa failed to realize that by giving too much attention to pass master Blanchflower they were leaving other Spurs players freedom, and unmarked Terry Dyson made it 2-0 with one of his typical dash-and-deliver runs that made him such a valuable asset to the Tottenham forward line.

Belatedly, Villa got a penalty that was duly dispatched by spot-kick specialist Stan Lynn. But Spurs shut up shop and the victory signalled that they had amassed 50 points quicker than any other First Division team in history in the two-points-a-win era.

QUOTE – Bobby Smith: ❛This was just the victory we needed after our poor showing against Leicester, but we know it will be a completely different challenge in the Cup next week. We will really have to be on our toes because the Cup is all Villa have left.❜

TEAM AND SCORERS: Brown, Baker, Henry; Blanchflower, Norman, Mackay; Jones, White, Smith, Allen, Dyson. Goalscorers: Smith, Dyson.

February 18   Villa Park   Attendance: 65,474
ASTON VILLA 0, TOTTENHAM 2

CLIFF JONES gave further evidence that he had developed into one of the world's most dangerous wingers with the two goals that had Spurs marching on into the FA Cup quarter-finals. Villa were much less comfortable than in the League meeting on the same pitch seven days earlier, and in truth they were lucky not to have been given a much bigger hiding – thanks largely to Spurs taking their foot off the accelerator.

There were 15,000 more spectators than for the previous game, and they were treated to a master class by a Tottenham team at the peak of its form. They simply passed Villa to death, and their first goal in the 18th minute captured their absolute supremacy. The Villa defenders chased shadows as the ball travelled on a conveyor belt of passes before being delivered on a plate for Jones to score goal number one.

The Welsh Wizard collected his second goal midway through the first-half, hammering the ball past goalkeeper Geoff Sidebottom after the Villa defence had been dismantled by a series of quickly transferred passes involving the entire forward line.

Much to the frustration of the Villa fans and the aggravation of the Villa players, Spurs played an almost arrogant game of keep-ball in the second-half. The midfield maestros Blanchflower, White and Mackay were in their element, and were so much in control of the midfield territory that the Villa players must have felt like walk-on extras in an epic production starring Super Spurs.

QUOTE – Cliff Jones: 'I got the goals but it was a team triumph. There were times when we played better than in any match this season. Everybody is buzzing about the possibility of the Double, but we are just taking each game as it comes.'

TEAM AND SCORERS: Brown, Baker, Henry; Blanchflower, Norman, Mackay; Jones, White, Smith, Allen, Dyson. Goalscorers: Jones (2).

Art Turner
2010

Born Lingdale, Co. Durham, February 22 1933. Scored 176 goals in 271 League matches for Spurs after joining them from Chelsea in 1955. Wound down his League career with Brighton, his 18 goals in 31 matches helping them win the Fourth Division Championship in 1965.

He scored 13 goals in 15 appearances as England centre-forward, all but one of them in partnership with Jimmy Greaves.

In the Double season Bobby was top First Division marksman for Spurs with 28 goals and he netted in each of the successive FA Cup final victories.

He was never given the credit he deserved for his high level of skill. People seemed to think he was all brute force. Strength certainly played an important part in his game, and he used to make full use of his heavyweight physique. But he also had subtle touches and could lay off delicate passes.

Les Allen and, later, Jimmy Greaves fed off him. Smithy did not think he was in the game until he had let the goalkeeper know he was on the pitch by hammering into him at the earliest opportunity. This was in the days when forwards were allowed to make physical contact with goalkeepers. He would survive and thrive on skill alone in the modern game – but he would not be the same old Smithy without letting everybody know who was boss by a show of a strength. There have been few more effective centre-forwards in an England shirt.

First Division   White Hart Lane   Attendance 62,261
TOTTENHAM 1, WOLVES 1

WOLVES were Tottenham's closest challengers in the chasing pack, and their resolute manager Stan Cullis had not yet thrown in the towel. He played mind games before the kick-off by suggesting the pressure of hunting the League and Cup Double was weighing heavily on the Spurs players. This seemed a nonsense in the tenth minute when the ball went from Maurice Norman in the Tottenham goalmouth, to Blanchflower, to Mackay, Dyson and then Bobby Smith, who crashed the ball home for a breath-taking goal.

This was a goal in typical Spurs style, and the opposite to the way Wolves played the game. Cullis believed in route one, and the fact that they had scored a century of goals in four successive seasons during the 1950s gave strength to his argument that "the more times you have the ball in the opponents' penalty area, the more goalscoring chances you will create."

The hopes Wolves had of winning seemed to lessen when skipper Bill Slater went off with damaged ribs following a collision with the powerhouse that was Bobby Smith. This was four years before the football rulers had the sense to introduce a substitute rule. Slater bravely came back on after being strapped up and played gingerly on the wing.

As often happens when playing a handicapped team, it was Tottenham who lost their rhythm and midway through the first-half a rare mistake by Blanchflower allowed Ted Farmer in for an equaliser and his 22nd League goal in 21 games. Battling Wolves thoroughly deserved their point.

QUOTE – Stan Cullis: ⁶Tottenham are clearly favourites to take the League title, but they also have eyes on the FA Cup and they could yet fall between the two. They now have a lot of psychological pressure, and it is up to all the chasing teams to show that the title race is far from over.⁹

TEAM AND SCORERS: Brown, Baker, Henry; Blanchflower, Norman, Mackay; Jones, White, Smith, Allen, Dyson. Goalscorer: Smith.

First Division   Maine Road   Attendance 40,278
MANCHESTER CITY 0, TOTTENHAM 1

THIS match pitched against each other two of the greatest Scottish footballers ever to grace the English soccer stage – Denis Law and Dave Mackay. Law had joined Man City from Huddersfield for what was then a record £53,000 (today he would be worth £53 million). Almost single handed, he was making City a power in the First Division, but waiting for him in this crucial battle at Maine Road was the one and only Dave Mackay, the braveheart of the Spurs.

It was Law who had the better of the duel with Mackay in the first-half, playing here, there and everywhere as he tried to find a way through the Tottenham defence in which Tony Marchi was doing a solid job deputising at centre-half for the injured Maurice Norman.

As the Maine Road pitch became a skating rink under a river of rain, Mackay started to cut down on Law's freedom, and in the second-half Tottenham were continually in the ascendancy.

They picked up the pace and the pressure and the goal they deserved came on the hour. Terry Medwin, deputising for Cliff Jones, sprinted past his marker to meet an inch-perfect centre from Danny Blanchflower, heading the ball into the City net off a post.

Tottenham were content to concentrate on contain and counter tactics as they cruised through the last half hour for a win that was much more emphatic than the scoreline suggests.

QUOTE – Denis Law: •During my career I was lucky to play with and against some of the best post-war teams. I can state quite categorically that Tottenham were up there with the best of them. They had all-round strength and skill, and each of their players was comfortable and confident on the ball.•

TEAM AND SCORERS: Brown, Baker, Henry; Blanchflower, Marchi, Mackay; Medwin, White, Smith, Allen, Dyson. Goalscorer: Medwin

March 4   Roker Park   Attendance: 61,236
SUNDERLAND 1, TOTTENHAM 1

ROKER PARK was heaving with a sell-out all-ticket crowd. The magic of the Cup had grabbed the Sunderland supporters, who were excited by the potential of their team who had lost only one of 20 Second Division games during the run up to their Cup challenge. Arsenal had fallen at Roker, and the young Sunderland team had seen off Liverpool and Norwich City in away Cup ties.

The Roker Roar was briefly silenced when the fit-again Cliff Jones scored one of his typical goals in the ninth minute, but the North East fans got behind their heroes and were like a 12th man as they screamed their encouragement.

Sunderland's goal survived several scares before they pulled level four minutes into the second-half. They forced three corners in quick succession, and the hectic, non-stop pressure eventually brought an equaliser from 18-year-old inside-left Willie McPheat after centre-half Charlie Hurley had beaten Maurice Norman in a high-jumping duel.

Suddenly the Double was looking doubtful as Sunderland came rushing forward, unleashing an avalanche of attacks. It took all of Danny Blanchflower's famous coolness to discipline a defence that was buckling. The Sunderland hurricane gradually eased as young legs became tired, and Tottenham managed to weather the storm. By the end of a memorable match Spurs were in control and you could sense Sunderland's best chance of causing a massive upset had gone.

QUOTE – Danny Blanchflower: ‘I have never known a crowd atmosphere like the one here at Roker. I could not hear myself think, let alone shout instructions. We were very relieved to hear that final whistle and to still be in the competition.’

TEAM AND SCORERS: Brown, Baker, Henry; Blanchflower, Norman, Mackay; Jones, White, Smith, Allen, Dyson. Goalscorer: Jones.

Art Turner
2010

Born Dagenham, Essex, September 4 1937. Scored 47 goals in 119 League matches for Spurs. Started his career as an amateur with Briggs Sports while working as an apprentice with the local Ford factory. Signed for Chelsea in 1954 and netted 11 goals in 44 League appearances before joining Tottenham in December 1959.

Making way for the arrival of Jimmy Greaves, he joined Queens Park Rangers and helped them become the first Third Division side to win the League Cup at Wembley. He scored 55 goals in 128 League games for QPR.

The Allen family are famous for their footballing feats. There was Les and his brother Dennis, and then Les's sons Clive and Bradley and nephews Martin and Paul. All became professionals. Bobby Smith had a prolific partnership with Allen, and together they played a major part in clinching the League and Cup double triumph. Les was a neat, constructive centre-forward or inside-forward with a fine turn of speed, an accurate right foot shot, and excellent positional sense. He was unlucky not to get international recognition, and also unlucky to have Jimmy Greaves around at the same time, both at Chelsea and Spurs. He managed QPR and Swindon before a spell in Greece in charge of Salonika. Les later became a skilled model maker, and in retirement shared his time between his homes in Essex and Cyprus. His son, Clive, became a Spurs legend.

FA CUP, Quarter-final replay

March 8   White Hart Lane   Attendance: 64,797
TOTTENHAM 5, SUNDERLAND 0

VETERAN Tottenham fans who were there remember this FA Cup quarter-final replay as one of the craziest yet most exciting nights ever at White Hart Lane. Thousands, including many ticket holders, were locked out, and several Tottenham players only made it to the ground just in time for the kick-off. Bobby Smith abandoned his car and finished the journey on the back of a police motor cycle.

It was just as crowded in the Sunderland penalty area as Tottenham put them in their place with an exhibition of attacking football at its most polished and potent.

Super Spurs were three goals clear at half-time and cantering towards the semi-finals. Les Allen scored with a thunderous shot after 27 minutes, and Bobby Smith made it 2-0 four minutes later after goalkeepr Peter Wakeham had failed to hold on to a Cliff Jones shot. Dyson added a third from a Jones centre in the dying moments of a first-half in which Sunderland were rushed off their feet.

Sunderland skipper Stan Anderson was an attacking right-half almost in the Blanchflower class, but he had to work overtime helping out his beleaguered defence. They cracked again in the 65th minute when Les Allen danced and dribbled his way past four challenges before releasing the ball for Dyson to collect his second goal.

Five minutes later the buccaneering Mackay picked his spot and cracked in goal number five with his lethal left foot. The jam-packed crowd were delirious.

QUOTE – Bill Nicholson: ʻWe have Burnley between us and the final at Wembley. They are the reigning League champions and an outstanding team. We still have it all to do.ʼ

TEAM AND SCORERS: Brown, Baker, Henry; Blanchflower, Norman, Mackay; Jones, White, Smith, Allen, Dyson. Goalscorers: Allen, Smith, Dyson (2), Mackay.

First Division   Ninian Park   Attendance: 45,463
CARDIFF CITY 3, TOTTENHAM 2

FROM the high of reaching the FA Cup semi-final Spurs crashed to a low of losing to a Cardiff City team that twice came back from a goal behind to win a match in which Tottenham were punished for casual and careless defensive play.

The game was switched to the Saturday evening because Wales were playing in a rugby international at Cardiff Arms Park, and when they beat Ireland by nine points to nil Danny Blanchflower said, prophetically: "This will get the crowd up. Every Welshman's passion is raised by a rugby victory." Cliff Jones, son of Swansea, nodded his agreement.

Terry Dyson quickly stifled the Welsh cheers when he snatched a third minute goal, and then seven minutes later City outside-left Derek Hogg was given unexpected time and space to pick his spot for an equaliser.

A neatly taken goal by Les Allen restored the Spurs lead, but they were lethargic at the start of the second-half and paid for their poor discipline by conceding goals by Brian Walsh and Derek Tapscott.

As Blanchflower had predicted, there was a special spirit surging through the Cardiff crowd that lifted their players to superhuman efforts, and they held out under a barrage of Tottenham attacks in a frantic final 20 minutes. Spectators rushed on to the pitch at the final whistle and hailed the Cardiff players as if they had just won the FA Cup. What they had achieved is a victory over Tottenham for the first time in Cardiff. Suddenly the Tottenham lead at the top of the table was not looking so emphatic.

QUOTE – Bill Nicholson: ʻThis was one of our worst defensive displays of the season, and we got what we deserved. I have been doing my best to play down talk of the Double and I am not going to discuss it now. I will only talk about football not fantasy.ʼ

TEAM AND SCORERS: Brown, Baker, Henry; Blanchflower, Norman, Mackay; Jones, White, Smith, Allen, Dyson. Goalscorers: Dyson, Allen

March 18   Villa Park   Attendance: 69,968
TOTTENHAM 3, BURNLEY 0

IT looked a potential classic on paper, League leaders Tottenham against League champions Burnley in the semi-final of the FA Cup. But on the pitch it proved something of a damp squib, mainly because the Lancastrians were not allowed to find their shape and rhythm by a Spurs side in determined mood to make it to Wembley.

Tottenham fans with good memories were nervous, because Spurs had lost their last three FA Cup semi-finals at Villa Park, but while Burnley had much of the territorial advantage in the first-half they were not allowed to trouble goalkeeper Bill Brown as Peter Baker, Ron Henry and Maurice Norman each played to the peak of their powers.

It was a rare mistake by Burnley skipper Jimmy Admason that let Spurs in for a nerve-settling opening goal on the half hour. Bobby Smith beat goalkeeper Adam Blacklaw with a rising shot after Adamson had lost control of the ball. Spurs should have had a penalty just before half-time when the referee failed to spot Burnley full-back John Angus punching out a Terry Dyson header.

Jimmy Robson had an equaliser ruled out early in the second-half because of a foul on Maurice Norman, and then Ron Henry was lucky to get away with handling the ball on the goalline. Smith knocked the wind out of Burnley with a crashing right foot shot in the 49th minute and Cliff Jones scored in the last minute to give the scoreline a flattering look. Wembley and the Double here we come!

QUOTE – Cliff Jones: ⁶For the first time in weeks Danny went back to his talk of the Double during the build-up to the semi-final. He convinced us that history was at our feet, and we went into the match absolutely determined to get the better of a very good Burnley side.⁹

TEAM AND SCORERS: Brown, Baker, Henry; Blanchflower, Norman, Mackay; Jones, White, Smith, Allen, Dyson. Goalscorers: Smith (2), Jones.

Art Turner
2010

Born Malton, North Yorkshire, November 29 1934. Played 184 League games for Spurs and scored 41 goals. He came to the Lane from non-League Scarborough in 1955, and was a member of the first-team squad until 1965 when he moved to Fulham and then Colchester and Guildford City.

A regular in the Double-winning side, he scored two goals that clinched victory in the European Cup-Winners' Cup final in 1963.

The son of famous jockey 'Ginger' Dyson, Terry had a heart as big as his head and would run his legs off for the team, and often popped up with vital winning goals. He had the most memorable match of his career in the European Cup-Winners' Cup final. He continually had the Atletico Madrid defence in disarray with his thrusting runs, and his two individually worked goals turned the match. He was big enough to admit he did not have the skill of some of those tremendous players around him, but he more than made up for it with his effort and atomic energy. Terry was equally effective on either wing. He managed non-League Dagenham and Boreham Wood, and later became an assessor of schoolboy footballers for the Football Association and worked as a PE teacher. In 1961 Terry became the first Tottenham player to score a hat-trick in the derby against Arsenal (Spurs won 4-3).

First Division   White Hart Lane   Attendance   46,470
TOTTENHAM 1, NEWCASTLE UNITED 2

THE euphoria at reaching the FA Cup final was replaced just four days later by edginess as Spurs slumped to a shock home defeat against a Newcastle side who were third from the bottom of the table and haunted by the threat of relegation. Suddenly the lead over Sheffield Wednesday at the top of the table had been cut to four points.

The astonishing fact is that Spurs could and should have been leading by at least six goals at half-time after battering the Newcastle defence in the most one-sided first-half witnessed at the Lane all season. They had to be content with just a 1-0 lead at half-time provided by Les Allen after inventive work by Cliff Jones on the right wing.

Goalkeeper Dave Hollins, brother of Chelsea's John, was making his Newcastle debut and made at least a dozen saves before Ivor Allchurch stole a stunning equaliser in the 64th minute.

Dramatically, the Tottenham players began to look tired as if all their effort of the last seven months had caught up with them. Bobby Smith was hobbling, and Dave Mackay and John White were looking ragged and not their usual dominating selves.

Newcastle could hardly believe they were getting out of jail when former Manchester United outside-left Albert Scanlon ended a counter-attack with a lob that caught Bill Brown out of position and helpless to stop the ball sailing into the net. Back-to-back League defeats for the first time in the season had Tottenham knees knocking.

QUOTE – Danny Blanchflower: ❛Anybody who witnessed this match will confirm it was a completely freak result. If we had scored ten goals it would have reflected our supremacy. We must keep our nerve, and be positive. The Double is very much on.❜

TEAM AND SCORERS: Brown, Baker, Henry; Blanchflower, Norman, Marchi; Jones, White, Smith, Allen, Dyson. Goalscorer: Allen.

First Division   Craven Cottage   Attendance   38,536
FULHAM 0, TOTTENHAM 0

NOW for something completely different – a goalless draw, the only time this scoreline featured throughout the Double season. Alarm bells were ringing in the Tottenham camp, because there was no question that the players were looking jaded and in need of a break just when their peak performances were required. They had now gone from February 25 since they had won a League match.

Even the usually indomitable Dave Mackay seemed to be almost burnt out, and he failed to control the menace of Fulham playmaker Johnny Haynes in a desperate scrap at Craven Cottage.

Luckily for Tottenham the probing passes from Haynes were not being converted into goals by team-mates who were not in his class. Schemer Haynes should have turned scorer twice in the second-half, but failed to find the net when clean through on goal.

The sudden nervousness of the Spurs players spread to their supporters, who were being reminded that the previous season it was successive home defeats by Chelsea and Manchester City that had stopped their chase for the championship over the Easter period.

As the final whistle blew at the Cottage the news came through that Sheffield Wednesday had crushed Manchester United 5-1. They were now just three points behind Tottenham, and there was widespread conjecture that the jinx of Double-chasing teams was about to descend on a Spurs side that was no longer looking in the Super category.

QUOTE – Terry Dyson: ˙The Boss didn't mince his words. He told us we were getting lazy and not focusing as we had earlier in the season. I don't think it was laziness as much as we were knackered. But we did need a kick up the arse, and Bill gave it to us.˙

TOTTENHAM TEAM: Brown, Baker, Henry; Blanchflower, Norman, Mackay; Jones, White, Smith, Allen, Dyson.

First Division   White Hart Lane   Attendance   65,032
TOTTENHAM 4, CHELSEA 2

THE Tottenham goal drought in the League stretched to 190 minutes after a goalless first-half against Chelsea in this Good Friday derby, and you could almost hear the sound of knocking knees on the terraces. Equally, there was a tsunami of relief when Cliff Jones carefully walked a Danny Blanchflower pass into the net two minutes into the second-half.

A weight had been lifted off the shoulders of the Tottenham players, and they sent Chelsea reeling with an avalanche of attacks that spawned goals from Jones again, Les Allen and Frank Saul, who was deputising for injured Bobby Smith.

Dave Mackay was also missing through injury, and Tony Marchi earned man-of-the-match ratings in the way he filled the great Mackay's shirt and kept a young Chelsea goalmaster called Jimmy Greaves on a tight leash.

Chelsea managed to add a little respectability to the scoreline with two late goals from Bobby Tambling and Ron Tindall, but the fact was that they had been outplayed by a Tottenham team who once again looked the part of champions in waiting.

Sheffield Wednesday were determined to try to take the title race down to the wire, and they kept three points behind with a 1-0 victory over Newcastle, who slipped to bottom place in the table on their way to relegation.

QUOTE – Les Allen: ‛This was a sweet victory against my old club. It restored our confidence just when people were starting to question whether we could win the championship, let alone the FA Cup. We were all aware of how the title had slipped out of our fingers with two defeats in the Easter period last season, and we were determined not to let that happen again.’

TEAM AND SCORERS: Brown, Baker, Henry; Blanchflower, Norman, Marchi; Jones, White, Saul, Allen, Dyson. Scorers: Jones (2), Allen, Saul

Art Turner 2010

Born Swansea, September 25 1932. Scored 65 goals in 197 League matches for Spurs between 1956 and 1962, after establishing himself as a Welsh international winger while with his hometown club, Swansea. He was capped 30 times by Wales and might have played many more games for Spurs but for a succession of injuries that finally forced his premature retirement after he had helped Tottenham retain the FA Cup at Wembley in 1962. Played 14 League games during the 'Double' campaign. He later became a top-flight coach, notably with Fulham.

Medwin came out of that marvellous Swansea finishing school that also produced players of the calibre of the Allchurch brothers, Mel Charles, Mel Nurse and, of course, Tottenham legend Cliff Jones. Terry was a very correct player, a student of the game who did everything with care and accuracy. His ball skill was of the highest order; he was always a menace to defences with his quick changes of pace, and he used to get up well to head the ball. It is a measure of the strength in depth of that Spurs squad that he was not a regular first-team player, yet was an automatic choice for Wales. He preferred to play on the right wing, which allowed his countryman Cliff Jones to feature in his favourite outside-left role. His cheerful personality made him a popular squad member, and he thoroughly deserved his Championship medal.

First Division   White Hart Lane   Attendance   46,325
TOTTENHAM 5, PRESTON 0

IT was once-proud Preston who were made to look the part of fools in this April 1 clash in which Tottenham carried on where they had left off against Chelsea the previous day. Preston were under siege from the third minute, when John White – recovering his early-season form – scored with a rare long-range shot that squeezed under the body of the diving goalkeeper Alan Kelly on a treacherously wet surface.

There were special celebrations for the second goal, steered deftly into the net by Cliff Jones following one of those sweeping pitch-length passing movements that had become a Tottenham trademark. The significance: this was the 100th League goal scored by Spurs since the first match back in August.

Frank Saul, looking more and more comfortable in the No 9 shirt, scored goal number 101, and then Danny Blanchflower completely fooled the Preston defenders with a dummied free-kick before passing the ball to Jones, who gleefully collected his second goal.

The fifth and final goal was a Cliff Jones exhibition piece as he completed his hat-trick with a stunning overhead kick. Poor Preston replaced Newcastle at the bottom of the table on their way down into the Second Division.

Sheffield Wednesday could only draw 1-1 against Blackburn Rovers at Ewood Park, and now no bookmakers would accept bets on Tottenham winning the title.

QUOTE – Cliff Jones: *'We have put our loss of form behind us, and our confidence is sky-high again. Obviously I am pleased with my hat-trick, but more pleased that the team is really ticking again. Everybody is now talking openly about the possibility of the Double, and we cannot wait for the final. It should be a cracker.'*

TEAM AND SCORERS: Brown, Baker, Henry; Blanchflower, Norman, Marchi; Jones, White, Saul, Allen, Dyson. Scorers: White, Jones (3), Saul

First Division   Stamford Bridge   Attendance 57,103
CHELSEA 2, TOTTENHAM 3

CHELSEA gave Spurs a scare before losing a five-goal thriller, and as Sheffield Wednesday dropped a point against Newcastle it was odds-on the title coming to White Hart Lane. This Bank Holiday Monday victory meant Tottenham had taken a maximum six points from their three Easter matches and silenced the critics doubting their staying power.

Bobby Smith – looking back to his swashbuckling best – had vowed to get a goal against the club that had let him go, and he put action where his mouth was in the seventh minute with a thumping header.

The odds on Tottenham winning shortened when Chelsea winger Peter Brabrook went off in the 34th minute after dislocating his shoulder in a collision with Maurice Norman. But the ten men of Chelsea gritted their teeth and made a battle of it. Jimmy Greaves celebrated what he thought was an equaliser until the referee ruled one of his team-mates had been off-side. Greavsie was booked for disputing the decision. Frank Blunstone pulled Chelsea level three minutes after half-time, and then Greaves made one of his typical runs from the halfway line and slotted the ball wide of Bill Brown to put Chelsea 2-1 in the lead. Jimmy played with a secret: He was on his way to Milan at the end of the season.

Tottenham showed they had character to go with their class following the Greaves goal. They dug deep to draw level through Terry Medwin. It was an eventful match for gentle giant Maurice Norman, who celebrated his recent wedding by heading in a Dave Mackay free-kick for a vital winning goal.

QUOTE – Maurice Norman: ⁶It has been an Easter I will never forget. My wedding, three victories and then getting the winning goal against Chelsea. The title is nearly ours.⁹

TEAM AND SCORERS: Brown, Baker, Henry; Blanchflower, Norman, Mackay; Medwin, White, Smith, Allen, Dyson. Goalscorers: Smith, Medwin, Norman

First Division   St Andrews   Attendance 40,961
BIRMINGHAM CITY 2, TOTTENHAM 3

THE fear factor of a month before had now been replaced by something of the old arrogance and swagger, and Spurs went about quickly putting Birmingham to the sword. The match was barely a minute old when they took the lead, forcing a corner from which John White headed against the bar, with Bobby Smith forcing in the rebound.

During a wave of attacks, John White had a perfectly good looking goal disallowed for off-side, and then – ironically – they scored their second goal through Les Allen, who tapped in a centre from a clearly off-side Bobby Smith. The non-stop blitz continued, and John White made it 3-0 after a mix up in the battered Birmingham defence.

In a rare City raid in the 39th minute, schemer Jimmy Bloomfield was upended and Jimmy Harris placed the ball for the spot-kick. He hammered the ball wide, but the referee ruled that it should be retaken because Bill Brown had moved. Harris made no mistake at the second time of asking. The half-time scoreline read 3-1, when it could so easily have been 8-1.

Two minutes after the interval Harris scored a second goal when he got on the end of a through ball from Bloomfield and guided the ball wide of the approaching Brown.

With Danny Blanchflower curbing his natural attacking instincts to help out in defence, Tottenham suffocated the Birmingham revival. The Spurs players and fans were delighted when they heard Sheffield Wednesday, the only team that could beat them to the title, had dropped another point at home to Leicester City.

QUOTE – Danny Blanchflower: 'Our destiny is now in our hands. We know that if we can beat Sheffield Wednesday in our next match the championship is ours.'

TEAM AND SCORERS: Brown, Baker, Henry; Blanchflower, Norman, Mackay; Jones, White, Smith, Allen, Dyson. Goalscorers: Smith, Allen, White

MONDAY, APRIL 17th, 1961

COPYRIGHT

VOL. LIII. NO. 47

ALL RIGHTS RESERVED

Chairman:
FRED. J. BEARMAN

Vice-Chairman:
FREDK. WALE

Directors:
F. JOHN BEARMAN, D. H. DEACOCK
S. A. WALE

Secretary:
R. S. JARVIS

Manager:
W. E. NICHOLSON

Medical Officer:
Dr. A. E. TUGHAN

TOTTENHAM HOTSPUR

FOOTBALL AND ATHLETIC COMPANY LIMITED

Official Programme

AND RECORD OF THE CLUB

VISIT OF SHEFFIELD WEDNESDAY

THIS evening we give a hearty welcome to Sheffield Wednesday in what is a vital fixture to both clubs in the League campaign now reaching its climax. It will be recalled that the Wednesday were the first team to defeat us this season when they won by 2 goals to 1 at Hillsborough on November 12th, and they have been in close attendance on us in the League table throughout the season, with the gap fluctuating at times with the fortunes of the clubs.

A feature of Sheffield Wednesday's performances this season has been the strength of their defence; they have conceded only 39 goals in 38 League games, a record which speaks for itself, and which represents the smallest debit total in the League. Only four times have they had more than two goals scored against them, and they won two of those matches by defeating Blackburn Rovers 5—4 at Hillsborough and Burnley 4—3 at Turf Moor.

Wednesday's away record also stamps them as a side to be accorded great respect. They have lost only three times on opponents' grounds, winning seven and drawing eight of their other 15 engagements. Their defeats were at Leicester (1—2), Wolverhampton (1—4), and Everton (2—4), with drawn games at Birmingham, West Ham, Manchester City, Blackburn and Arsenal (all 1—1). In addition to their victory at Burnley already mentioned, they have won at Cardiff, Blackpool, Bolton and Newcastle (all 1—0), Nottingham Forest (2—1) and Fulham (6—1).

The defeat at Everton on December 3rd was actually their last in a League match; since then they have gone through 19 First Division fixtures without a reverse. Their performance in doing so is all the more meritorious when it is recalled that they were involved in a coach crash on Boxing Day on their way home from Arsenal to Sheffield. Several of their players, including Peter Swan and Bobby Craig, were injured and a young reserve forward, Douglas McMillan, had to have a leg amputated. Swan received a shoulder injury which kept him out of the game for the next nine League and Cup games.

There are two ever-presents in the Hillsborough side's defence in right-back Peter Johnson and left-half Tony Kay, while right-half Tommy McAnearney has missed only two games and left-back Don Megson four, all through injury. Swan has been absent from six League matches, and goalkeeper Ron Springett—who has missed four First Division games. In the attack, skipper Alan Finney has a full attendance record; he has played on both flanks of the attack, his last eight appearances having been at outside-right. At centre-forward, Keith Ellis has been the most regular choice. Three members of the attack have reached double figures as marksmen, with inside-left John Fantham leading the way with 19 League goals. Ellis has scored 14 times and Craig 12. Finney has five goals to his name, and Derek Wilkinson, who has played at outside-left in the last seven matches, after a spell on the other wing, has scored twice.

The Wednesday's last League defeat, on December 3rd, was their third reverse in consecutive games; on

---

In the Interests of Ground Conditions, Players on either side will not sign Autographs on the Field

Printed by Thomas Knight & Co. Ltd.,
The Clock House Press, Hoddesdon, Herts

PRICE TWOPENCE

The Sheffield Wednesday match programme from the A1Sporting Memorabilia collection

First Division   White Hart Lane   Attendance 61,205
TOTTENHAM 2, SHEFFIELD WEDNESDAY 1

A PAINFUL thing happened to Spurs braveheart Dave Mackay on his way to the crucial Monday night League championship showdown with Sheffield Wednesday. On the Saturday he was in the Scotland team savaged 9-3 by England at Wembley, a mauling that included three goals by Jimmy Greaves and two by Bobby Smith. For Mackay, it was hardly the best preparation for a game in which Spurs could clinch the title.

Nerves were jangling and the midfield trio of Blanchflower, White and Mackay were unusually subdued. The Tottenham fans roared their disapproval as referee Tommy Dawes awarded Wednesday a 19th minute free-kick when John Fantham tripped over his own feet. Left-back Don Megson crashed the free-kick against the Tottenham wall, and then instinctively drove the rebound wide of diving goalkeeper Bill Brown.

Just as it looked as if Spurs were going to trudge into the half-time interval trailing to the only team that could snatch the championship from them they touched the majestic peak of their power. A 35-yard clearance by Peter Baker was headed on by Terry Dyson to Bobby Smith, who spun around his close-marking England team-mate Peter Swan and hammered a rising shot into the net for a spectacular goal. With seconds to go to half-time, Les Allen made it 2-1 when he scored from 15 yards after Maurice Norman had headed a Blanchflower free-kick down to his feet.

Shell-shocked Wednesday were not allowed back into the game, and for an hour after the match the Tottenham fans sung their glory-glory anthems as the players paraded in the main stand.

QUOTE – Danny Blanchflower: ⁶One down, one to go. I am feeling confident that I will be saying to our chairman Fred Bearman, 'I told you so.' But we must be careful not to take anything for granted.⁹

TEAM AND SCORERS: Brown, Baker, Henry; Blanchflower, Norman, Mackay; Jones, White, Smith, Allen, Dyson. Scorers: Smith, Allen

ASK any Tottenham fan with knowledge of the club's glorious past to name the Double team and they will reel off the players like old friends: Brown, Baker, Henry, Blanchflower, Norman, Mackay, Jones (Medwin), White, Smith, Allen, Dyson. But five other players had more than walk-on parts in that unforgettable season ...

FRANK SAUL, Born Canvey Island, August 23, 1943. Frank deputised six times for Bobby Smith in the No 9 shirt, and contributed three goals to the haul of 115 First Division goals. Saul had his greatest moment in a Spurs shirt when he scored in the 2-1 1967 FA Cup final victory. Later played for Southampton, QPR and Millwall.

TONY MARCHI, Born Edmonton, January 21, 1933. Tony, whose 15-year Spurs career was interrupted by a two-year spell in Italy, played six matches in the Double team. He gained legendary status when filling in for Dave Mackay in the 1963 Cup Winners' Cup final. He later managed Cambridge City and Northampton Town.

JOHNNY HOLLOWBREAD, Born Ponders End, January 2, 1934. Johnny played just one match in the Double season, replacing injured Bill Brown in the 3-0 Boxing Day win over West Ham. Wound down his career with Southampton. He died in Spain on December 7 2007 at the age of 73.

KEN BARTON, Born Caernarfon, September 20, 1937. Ken made just one appearance at right-back in place of injured Peter Baker, the 2-0 defeat by Man United at Old Trafford. He later played briefly for Luton. Ken died on September 6 1982, aged 44.

JOHN SMITH, born Shoreditch, January 4, 1939. John was bought from West Ham as successor to Blanchflower, but he got only one chance to play in the Double season, taking over from Terry Medwin in the 2-0 defeat at Old Trafford. He later played for Coventry, Orient, Torquay, Swindon and Walsall. He was in the Swindon team that shocked Arsenal in the 1969 League Cup final. John died in 1988, aged 49.

First Division   Turf Moor   Attendance 28,991
BURNLEY 4, TOTTENHAM 2

WITH three League matches left after clinching the championship, Tottenham had one more target in their sights – the record First Division 66 points haul set by deadly North London rivals Arsenal, back in the dim and distant past when Herbert Chapman was in charge at Highbury.

But by the time they got to Turf Moor, to face the previous champions, Spurs were almost literally out on their feet. Completely against the run of play, Tottenham stole a 2-0 first-half lead. Peter Baker scored his one and only goal of the season with a long-range shot that shocked him as much as goalkeeper Adam Blacklaw when it flashed into the Burnley net. Bobby Smith added the second goal after a long spell of Burnley pressure, heading the ball home from a lobbed centre from Terry Dyson.

It was a mystery to everybody watching the game how Tottenham had managed to get a commanding lead when nearly all the attacking had come from a Burnley team for whom the two Jimmys – Adamson and McIlroy – were bossing the midfield.

Perhaps the Spurs players had overdone their League title triumph celebrations, but they looked tired and tortured throughout the second-half as Burnley blitzed them with non-stop attacks. Gordon Harris scored twice, McIlroy got on the scoresheet and created a fourth goal as Spurs were made to look chumps rather than champs. But for a series of exceptional saves by Bill Brown the Burnley score might easily have been doubled.

QUOTE – Peter Baker: ‘I was so pleased to find the net, but am disappointed that it did not help us win the match. I think we have all been hit by a feeling of anti-climax after that great night against Sheffield Wednesday.’

TEAM AND SCORERS: Brown, Baker, Henry; Blanchflower, Norman, Mackay; Jones, White, Smith, Allen, Dyson. Scorers: Baker, Smith

League Match 41: *April 26 1961*

First Division   White Hart Lane   Attendance 35,753
TOTTENHAM 1, NOTTINGHAM FOREST 0

A RARE 1-0 victory brought Tottenham level with Arsenal on the record First Division points haul of 66 points, with one game still to go. This Wednesday evening game even tested the stamina of the Tottenham fans, with 'only' 35,753 getting along to watch a Nottingham Forest side that had decided to put its faith at the feet of a squad of young, home-bred players.

Tottenham continued where they left off at Burnley, playing without their usual zeal and skill. It was a fairly unanimous verdict that this was one of their loosest and laziest performances of the season, and Bill Nicholson gave them a roasting after a goalless first-half. Only some desperate defending and more agile work on the goal-line by Bill Brown stopped Forest from scoring at least three goals before Spurs at last got the ball into the net.

What proved the only goal of a disappointing match came from the one player in the Spurs team who would not make the line-up for the FA Cup final at Wembley – Terry Medwin, the ever-cheerful and faithful winger who had spent the entire season on standby and occasional active duty in place of either Cliff Jones or Terry Dyson.

Spurs slogged rather than purred forward to get behind the disciplined Forest defence, and Medwin came scampering through to scoop the ball past highly rated Nottingham goalkeeper Peter Grummitt. Few but the one-eyed thought Tottenham deserved to take both points.

QUOTE – Bill Nicholson: 'This was a very disappointing performance. I am so proud of what the team has achieved this season, but this was an unacceptable slip in our standards. To compensate our supporters, I hope we can overtake the Arsenal points record in our final game.'

TEAM AND SCORERS: Brown, Baker, Henry; Blanchflower, Norman, Mackay; Medwin, White, Smith, Allen, Dyson. Goalscorer: Medwin

First Division   White Hart Lane   Attendance 52,054
TOTTENHAM 1, WEST BROMWICH ALBION 2

PHYSICALLY, Tottenham's players were at White Hart Lane for this final League game of the season, but their minds were clearly fourteen miles away at Wembley. The record of 66 points – set by Arsenal in 1931 and equalled by Spurs in 1961 – was there to be taken. But, to all-round disappointment and frustration, they failed to beat it.

For the second successive match Bill Nicholson found himself having to make blistering criticisms after a goalless first-half during which middle-of-the-table West Brom looked the most likely to score.

It looked as if the Nicholson rocket had done the trick four minutes into the second-half when Bobby Smith – with the Albion players appealing for off-side – found the net for his 28th League goal of the season.

But West Brom quickly drew level when Derek Kevan – one of Bobby Smith's rivals for the No 9 England shirt – bullocked his way through the Tottenham defence to get on the end of a Clive Clark centre and power it past Bill Brown.

The winning goal came in the 62nd minute from the right foot of one Bobby Robson, who surprised Bill Brown with a snap shot from 25 yards that hit the back of the net with the Tottenham goalkeeper able only to wave to it as it whooshed past him. Robson, equally at home in midfield or as a support striker, was into the fifth of six years with Albion before returning to his first club, Fulham, in 1962.

QUOTE – Bobby Robson: ❛Nobody can deny that we deserved both points today, but we are realistic enough to know we beat a below-par Tottenham team who were clearly playing with their minds on the Cup final and the Double. I will be amazed if they don't win the Cup to go with the League title. They are a fantastic team.❜

TEAM AND SCORERS: Brown, Baker, Henry; Blanchflower, Norman, Mackay; Jones, White, Smith, Allen, Dyson. Goalscorer: Smith

FINAL FIRST DIVISION TABLE, 1960-61

	P	HW	HD	HL	HGF	HGA	AW	AD	AL	AGF	AGA	Points	G Avg
Tottenham	42	15	3	3	65	28	16	1	4	50	27	66	.0909
Sheff Wed	42	15	4	2	45	17	8	8	5	33	30	58	.6595
Wolves	42	17	2	2	61	32	8	5	8	42	43	57	.3733
Burnley	42	11	4	6	58	40	11	3	7	44	37	51	.3246
Everton	42	13	4	4	47	23	9	2	10	40	46	50	.2608
Leicester C.	42	12	4	5	54	31	6	5	10	33	39	45	.2428
Man Utd	42	14	5	2	58	20	4	4	13	30	56	45	.1578
Blackburn	42	12	3	6	48	34	3	6	11	29	42	43	.0131
Aston Villa	42	13	3	5	48	28	4	6	11	30	49	43	.0129
West Brom	42	10	3	8	43	32	8	2	11	24	39	41	.9436
Arsenal	42	12	3	6	44	35	3	8	10	33	50	41	.9058
Chelsea	42	10	5	6	61	48	5	2	14	37	52	37	.98
Man City	42	10	5	6	41	30	3	6	12	38	60	37	.8777
Nottm Forest	42	8	7	6	34	33	6	2	13	28	45	37	.7948
Cardiff C.	42	11	5	5	34	26	2	6	13	26	59	37	.7058
West Ham	42	12	4	5	53	31	1	6	14	24	57	36	.875
Fulham	42	8	8	5	39	39	6	0	15	33	56	36	.7578
Bolton	42	9	5	7	38	29	3	6	12	20	44	35	.7945
Birmingham	42	10	4	7	35	31	4	2	15	27	53	34	.7380
Blackpool	42	9	3	9	44	34	3	6	12	24	39	33	.9315
Newcastle	42	7	7	7	51	49	4	3	14	35	60	32	.7889
Preston	42	7	6	8	28	25	3	4	14	15	46	30	.6056

Note: In the original English Division 1 (old) 1960-61 goal average applied instead of goal difference

*From the authors' scrapbook, 50 years old – an autographed
magazine picture of Danny Blanchflower with the League
Championship trophy*

THERE was just one theme on the minds of almost everybody in English football in the week leading up to Tottenham's FA Cup final showdown with Leicester City at Wembley: The Double. Spurs had won the League championship in style, despite a few hiccups. Now the topic in pubs and clubs throughout the land was whether they could achieve 'the impossible dream' and do what no other team in the 20th Century had managed – add the FA Cup to the collection.

The other twenty First Division managers not involved in the final were asked their opinions. This is what they had to say:

HARRY CATTERICK (manager of runners-up Sheffield Wednesday, who was shortly to switch to Everton): ʻThe mind plays funny games in football. On the face of it, Leicester should not have a chance. But there will be enormous pressure on the Tottenham players to produce the goods, and it just might stop them playing their usual composed and controlled football. I think much depends on what freedom Danny Blanchflower can find. He is the key player. If he can take control of the midfield then Leciester just might find themselves pulled apart. I am going for a Tottenham win, but it may not be the easy job that a lot of people are predicting.ʼ

STAN CULLIS (manager of third-place Wolves): ʻWe have been within touching distance of the Double on three occasions, and so I can vouch that it becomes as much a psychological barrier as a physical one. If Tottenham can play to the peak that had the League title virtually in the bag by Christmas, then I don't see how Leicester can live with them. But in the last few weeks there have been signs that they have lost that early-season confidence. It all depends on how the Spurs players react when they come out on to that Wembley pitch. It is a vast stadium and the atmosphere can either inflate or deflate a player's confidence. I go for a Tottenham win, but would not be too surprised if there is an upset.ʼ

HARRY POTTS (manager of fourth-placed Burnley): 'I am a great admirer of Spurs manager Bill Nicholson and the football that his team play. It is beautiful to watch, even when you are on the receiving end . We were desperately disappointed that we were unable to retain the championship this season, but I bow the knee to Tottenham. They thoroughly deserved to take the title, and I believe we will see history made at Wembley, with Spurs completing that elusive Double. Leicester are a good workmanlike team, who have a solid defence and they can produce moments of magic. But they lack Tottenham's consistency and class. I will be astonished if they beat Tottenham, but this is football and anything can happen. My prediction is an emphatic victory for Tottenham by a clear two or three goals.'

JOHNNY CAREY (manager of fifth-placed Everton, soon to be sacked during a cab ride with his club chairman; the start of the 'taxi' chant from fans whenever a manager is under threat): 'I have no hesitation in saying that Tottenham will beat Leicester and so clinch the Double. I think Spurs simply have too much fire power. Just look at their goals record this season, 115 and scored against some of the best defences in the country. Leicester are capable of playing some excellent football, but they tend to blow hot and cold, while Tottenham's is a consistent heat. I think the Wembley surface will suit Tottenham's style. They play purists football and I think the game will show British football in its best light. I think I will be telephoning that fine manager Bill Nicholson and congratulating him on completing the Double.'

MATT BUSBY (manager of seventh-placed Manchester United): 'I have been in the game far too long to be drawn into making predictions. What I will say is that if any team deserves to be first to achieve the Double it is Tottenham. They play football with the heart as well as the mind, and it is a reflection of how their solid and reliable manager Bill Nicholson thinks about the game. But don't make the mistake of just writing Leicester City off. They have played some excellent football on occasions this season, and if they can play to the top of their form they could give Tottenham a very difficult afternoon. Here at United we have experienced what it is like to have the Double within our sights and the pressure that brings with it. No prediction, then, but just let's say I will be surprised if the hot favourites do not win. But you only have to look at recent history to know that anything can happen at Wembley – anything.'

JACK MARSHALL (manager of eighth-placed Blackburn Rovers): 'As Tottenham hammered us with four goals away and five at home you will not be surprised to learn that I am predicting that they will not only complete the Double but do it in style. They have consistently been the outstanding team in the First Division this season, and if they get anywhere near their best form I do not see how Leicester can live with them. We were beaten by Wolves in last year's final at the end of a season in which they just missed the Double. I think this Tottenham team is even more efficient than that Wolves side, and they play a different sort of passing game. With Wolves, you had to beware their long balls pumped continually into the penalty area, while Spurs are more sophisticated but just as potent.'

JOE MERCER (manager of ninth-placed Aston Villa): 'Tottenham broke our hearts in the fifth round, and I told Bill Nicholson after the match that I thought he had every chance to go on and win the Cup. I still hold that opinion because I think they simply have too much all-round ammunition for Leicester. They beat us three times this season, scoring ten goals to our three, so you could say they have earned our full respect. Danny Blanchflower, who they stole from us, has had an incredible season and is the player who pulls the strings along with the under-rated John White who is a real players' player. Then there is that powerful competitor Dave Mackay completing one of the finest midfield trios in the modern game. Billy Nick has got the balance of his team just right, and I cannot see Leicester being able to cope with their sweeping attacks.'

GORDON CLARK (manager of tenth-placed West Bromwich Albion): 'I think we proved in the last League game of the season that nothing is certain in football. Nobody gave us a chance of winning at White Hart Lane against a Tottenham team that needed just a draw to set a new all-time First Division points record. But we managed to beat them 2-1 against all the odds. I am sure Leicester manager Matt Gillies will be hammering home the fact to his players that Tottenham are not unbeatable, as we proved. But if you put a gun to my head I would have to pick Tottenham as the likely winners. We are realistic enough to know that the team we beat did not have their mind fully on the game. They already had the title sewn up, and you could almost see some of their players thinking of Wembley. I have always been a fan of the way Spurs play the game, and if they do get the Double it will be pure football that is the winner.'

John White, the players' player according to Aston Villa manager Joe Mercer

GEORGE SWINDIN (manager of eleventh-placed Arsenal): 'I will probably get strung up by Arsenal supporters for saying this, but I rate this Tottenham Hotspur team as good as we have seen in post-war football. They scored seven goals in their two matches against us this season, and I am honest enough to accept that they are the superior side at the moment, but I am confident we will be back on top soon! A lot will depend at Wembley on how Leicester choose to play. If they adopt a cautious attitude and play defensively then they could get taken apart. But there are some question marks about Tottenham's defence under pressure. Everybody talks about the 115 goals that they have scored in the League, but don't forget they have conceded 55, and they can be vulnerable against quick counter attacks. It will be interesting to see if Leicester can stretch them.'

TED DRAKE (manager of twelfth-placed Chelsea): 'It will be the shock of the season if Leicester can beat Tottenham, but strange things often happen in football. It's the unpredictability that makes it such a compelling game. If I was a betting man I would have a punt on Leicester. They are the underdogs with nothing to lose, and can relax and play their natural game. Tottenham have this cross that they have been carrying for much of the season, the Double. I bet Billy Nicholson is sick to death of the mention of it. But being realistic, I have to say everything points to a comfortable win for Tottenham. Let's face it, they are a class side and in Bobby Smith and Les Allen have an attacking partnership that can take any defence apart. Both of them learned their trade at Chelsea, and so they have been well educated!'

LES McDOWALL (manager of thirteenth-placed Manchester City): 'We were the first team this season to show that Tottenham could be held when we drew with them at White Hart Lane in October. Leicester's best chance of winning is to suffocate them in midfield. If you make a study of the Tottenham goals this season you will find that virtually everything emanates from the feet of either Danny Blanchflower or John White. If Leicester can stop the ball getting to them, then they just might be in with a shout. But common sense tells me that Spurs have too much all-round strength, and that they will probably win by at least two goals. Leicester are inconsistent, but in Gordon Banks they have a fine young goalkeeper and their defence doesn't take prisoners. They have some strong tacklers and so Tottenham cannot expect to be handed the Cup on a plate.'

ANDY BEATTIE (manager of fourteenth-placed Nottingham Forest): 'Leicester manager Matt Gillies is an old friend of mine and I have been telling him that the way to beat Tottenham is with high balls into the penalty area. There are often misunderstandings between goalkeeper Bill Brown and centre-half Maurice Norman, and if they can make them uncertain on that fast Wembley pitch then anything could happen. We had them unsettled at White Hart Lane recently, and Bill Nicholson admitted they were lucky to get away with both points. But having made out a case for how Leicester can win, I have to be honest and admit I just cannot see it. Blanchflower, White and Mackay are as formidable a midfield trio as there is in the game, and Cliff Jones has developed into a winger of true world class. If Leicester can snatch an early goal then anything is possible, but I am fully expecting to see Tottenham win with perhaps as many as three goals to spare.'

BILL JONES (manager of fifteenth-placed Cardiff City): 'Our first season back in the top flight has been a real eye opener and co-incided with Spurs emerging as one of the all-time great sides. We managed to give them two hard battles, losing 3-2 in the first match and then managing to beat them 3-2 at Ninian Park. My advice to Leicester would be to go for it. We took the game to Tottenham in Cardiff and often had their defence at sixes and sevens. But they are awesome coming forward, and I can't see how Leicester will be able to keep them out. I think it could be a high-scoring game, with Tottenham probably coming out on top because they have the greater firing power. Cliffie Jones is becoming a legend for Spurs and for Wales. Is there a quicker and braver winger? I don't think so.'

RON GREENWOOD (manager of sixteenth-placed West Ham): 'I have only just settled into the job here at West Ham, and I do not really feel as if I want to get involved in the forecasting game. My concentration is on building a team that can live with the likes of a great side like Tottenham over the next decade. While coaching at Arsenal I often found myself on courses with Bill Nicholson and I have enormous respect for him as a man and as a coach. There are few better tacticians in the world game, and I am sure he will have something worked out for the final that will negate anything that Leicester can come up with. On paper it obviously looks a good thing for Tottenham, but football has a habit of throwing up shocks in the FA Cup. I am a great fan of John White's style of football. He is an instinctive player who makes wonderful blindside runs that are not always appreciated by the fans. He just might be the hidden ace.'

Bill Brown, the goalkeeper whose composure spread calm to the players around him

BEDFORD JEZZARD (manager of seventeenth-placed Fulham): ❛Well, we were the only team to hold Tottenham to a goalless draw after getting a five-goal tanking at White Hart Lane. My advice to Leicester is to try to pack the midfield so that Blanchflower and White have restricted room. Give them space and they can take you apart with passes that are incisive and always accurate. Smith and Allen grab most of the goals, but it is Blanchflower and White who create the openings. Frank McLintock carries a lot of responsibility. He has good attacking instincts, and will have to play out of his skin if he is to get the better of the Blanchflower-White duo. It might not be the great spectacle people are expecting because the only chance Leicester have of winning is to stop Tottenham from playing. I have a hunch Spurs will win by just one goal.❜

BILL RIDDING (manager of eighteenth-placed Bolton Wanderers): ❛I'll be honest, I would love to see Tottenham win and win in style. They are a fine advertisement for English football with their sophisticated football that is as good as you see anywhere in Europe. The Double is a great incentive for them, and I think the smoothness of the Wembley pitch will suit their passing game. Billy Nicholson has a great football brain and I think he will come up with the tactics to counter anything Leicester might try to throw at them. There is class running all the way through the Tottenham team and I just can't see Leicester being able to live with them. Here at Bolton we play a much more physical game than Spurs, but I'm sure if I had players of the quality of Blanchflower, White, Mackay and Jones I would be adopting a different style.❜

GIL MERRICK (manager of nineteenth-placed Birmingham City): ❛Tottenham put nine goals into our net in two matches and so I have the utmost respect for them. We tried attacking them in the first game and came unstuck against the speed of their counter raids. We tried restricting their movement in the next match by man-to-man marking, and found ourselves leaving space that was exploited by players running through from deep positions. When they are on their game they are almost impossible to stop. As an ex-goalkeeper, I am an admirer of Bill Brown. He has his critics because he is sometimes hesitant on crosses, but he has a fine understanding with Maurice Norman and you rarely see them in trouble. Bill has an excellent temperament, and his composure spreads to the players around him. It would be a good boost for Midlands football if Leicester could follow Wolves and Forest as Cup winners, but I just cannot see it happening.❜

RONNIE SUART (manager of twentieth-placed Blackpool): 'Tottenham beat us twice in the opening weeks of the season, and I said to Bill Nicholson that he had the makings of a team good enough to win everything in sight. Now I expect them to finish off a historic season by winning the FA Cup to go with the League title. I will be delighted for Bill because he is a manager who always represents our game with dignity and honesty. And that's how his team plays. They do not cheat or bend the rules. Yes, Dave Mackay can tackle like a clap of thunder, but he is not dirty with it like some players I could name. Bill Nick's next boast will be his first, yet he has built a team for which he has plenty to boast about. I would put them up there with the Busby Babes as the finest English team since the war and every bit as good as the Arsenal side of the 1930s.'

CHARLIE MITTEN (manager of 21st and relegated Newcastle United): 'We offer some hope to Leicester becaue we were one of the few teams to beat Spurs this season, and on their own park at White Hart Lane. Leicester's players have to be ready to run their socks off to match the work-rate of Tottenham. That is one of the secrets of Spurs that rarely gets a mention. For all their skill and talent they have a team of players who are prepared to run their legs off. They work really hard for each other, and when you get this energy mixed with the sort of ball-playing skill they have then that is a winning combination. Let's face it, Leicester are not in their class and should not be in with a shout. But football is a strange old game, and odder things have happened. The FA Cup is never short of surprises, but it will be the shock of the century if Spurs lose this final.'

JIMMY MILNE (manager of 22nd and relegated Preston): 'I have good reason to respect Tottenham. On my first day in charge – on April the first of all days – they hammered us 5-0 at White Hart Lane, and I saw just why everybody in the game is raving about them. They are a formidable force without a single weakness, and I cannot think of many words of encouragement that I can offer to Leicester. The danger, of course, is that Tottenham could beat themselves by being over-confident. But I know the way Bill Nicholson manages, and there is no way he will allow even a hint of complacency. I used to play in midfield for Preston alongside Bill Shankly, and the way Blanchflower and Mackay play reminds me of the partnership I had with Shanks. Leicester must try to close them down in midfield. If they give them too much space they will run the game and Totenham will win with ease. To be frank, I do not give Leicester a hope.'

EVERYTHING in the last week of the season building to the FA Cup final was geared to making sure the Tottenham players relaxed. Each morning they reported to White Hart Lane for light warm-up sessions followed by tactical briefings from Bill Nicholson. This was the Spurs manager in his element. He ate, drank and slept football theories, and any time you sat at a meal table with him you knew that the salt, pepper and cutlery would finish up in a football formation.

On the Wednesday before the final the players were ordered to report to the training ground at Cheshunt. The groundsman had been working overtime preparing one of the outer pitches with a surface as close as possible to the famous green sward of Wembley. For two hours, the players went through the routines Nicholson had worked out. He encouraged input from the players, and Danny Blanchflower was – of course – the most vocal.

QUOTE – Danny Blanchflower: *Bill was very democratic and was happy to hear suggestions, but the final say on tactics were always his. But as captain I had the freedom to make changes on the pitch if and when I felt it was necessary. This off-the-cuff tactical responsibility got me in trouble in my early days at Tottenham, because the directors did not understand the game. They decided I was getting ideas above my station and it led to me spending some time on the transfer list, but once Bill became manager we agreed that it was a captain's job to make and take decisions in the heat of battle. We were confident that we had the right tactics to get the better of Leicester, and in that session at Cheshunt we all became familiar with our duties.*

A secret kept from the press was that three of the key players – Danny, Dave Mackay and Bobby Smith – were struggling with niggling injuries, and were spending a lot of time in the treatment room after the training and tactical sessions. Danny had a twisted right knee and bruised right ankle which required daily heat treatment, and he kept to himself that his father was slowly fading away after a long illness.

Bobby Smith's problem was a nagging knee injury that was often so painful he wondered if it was going to stop him playing in the FA Cup final, which in those days was the pinnacle of a professional footballer's career. He did not let on to the Tottenham medical staff just how serious the pain was for fear that Bill Nicholson would choose not to gamble on his fitness and bring in the young prospect Frank Saul.

Without telling a soul, Bobby made two top-secret visits to his local doctor on the morning of the game for painkiller injections in the knee – each time pretending he was going out for a stroll.

QUOTE – Bobby Smith: ‘I had dreamt all my footballing life of playing in an FA Cup final at Wembley, and I was determined not to miss out now after all the effort I had put into helping us get there. My family was coming down from the North-East and I did not want to let them down. Bill Nick would have shot me if he had known, but I made two private visits to my doctor in Palmers Green on the morning of the match to deaden the pain so that I could play.’

Dave Mackay had been trying to shake off a shin injury ever since the best forgotten match for Scotland against England at Wembley on April 15. Tony Marchi was put on standby, but this was one match that Dave was determined not to miss.

As well as fans mobbing the players wherever they went in the week of the final, they were also surrounded by ticket touts who were doing a brisk business at a time when the allocation for the clubs were around just 25,000 each. The Football Association considered the final a national event and tickets went to nationwide County Associations and were handed on to people who had little or no interest in the competing teams.

The new financial structure for footballers had yet to be introduced, so many of the players got involved in black-marketing their tickets. It was illegal, but was one of the few perks that the players had at the back-end of the soccer slave era. The likes of Johnny the Stick, One-Arm Lou and Fat Stan Flashman – they preferred to be called ticket agents rather than touts – made bundles of money from tickets passed on to them by players.

On the eve of the final, the Tottenham team booked into the vast Hendon Hall Hotel (also England's headquarters for the 1966 World Cup finals). They lunched together and then visited Wembley Stadium to get a feel of the famous old twin-

Bobby Smith injecting power into his challenge against Wolves goalkeeper Malcolm Finlayson in the days when players could shoulder-charge goalies without risking a yellow or red card.

towered ground that was the cathedral of English football.

As the players walked around the empty pitch it was not a sight particularly enjoyed by Dave Mackay, who considered the ground way down on his list of favourites. He had first played there for Scotland Under-15s against England in a schoolboy international in 1950. England, with Johnny Haynes their star, won 8-2. Then, just three weeks before this crucial final, he had been in the Scotland team slaughtered 9-3 by England, with a certain Johnny Haynes again pulling the strings in midfield.

An agency reporter among the press pack on the Wembley pitch was brave (or foolish) enough to ask Dave if he had got the England defeat out of his system.

QUOTE – Dave Mackay: ʻDon't mention the war! As far as I'm concerned that's a blanked out memory. Let's just say our goalkeeper had a game he would prefer to forget. The Cup final is a different game altogether, and previous matches will not come into my mind. With the great players we have in our side and our team spirit and understanding I am confident we can win the Cup. I have never been on a losing side in a cup final in my life.ʼ

Cliff Jones and John White, inseparable pals, played in front of one of the Wembley goals with a pretend ball and John White mimed as if shooting the ball into the net and then celebrating a goal.

"Knowing you and your finishing," said Cliff, "you will put the ball over the bar and out of the ground."

The Jones and White double act was popular with all the Tottenham players and staff. They were continually pulling each other's leg, and had been known to sword fight on dining tables and hang each other out of hotel windows shouting for help.

Bill Nick, like a concerned but loving father, used to have to often tell them to curb their clowning, but quietly he knew it was good for team spirit.

It was agreed that the Wembley pitch was looking in magnificent condition, and well suited to Tottenham's all-along-the-ground passing game. Terry Dyson, making his first playing visit to Wembley, said it seemed bigger than Hyde Park. Bill Nick quietly told him: "The more space the better for us. I wish we could play on a pitch like this every week. It is like a green carpet, ideal for our passing game."

That Friday evening, Nicholson led his troops on a visit to the cinema. They watched the *Guns of Navarone* at the Leicester Square Odeon. But the really big guns were going to be needed at Wembley the next day.

THE 1961 FA Cup final was as much a television event as a football fixture. The BBC had it to themselves, and started screening their all-day show from Wembley at 11.00 o'clock on the Saturday morning. David Coleman made his opening introduction from the Royal Box, and commentator Kenneth Wolstenholme interviewed early arrivals down Wembley Way. These were the early days of Eurovision television, and the match action would be seen live in more than a dozen countries.

Walley Barnes gave a pitch report from the spot where in the 1952 FA Cup final he had so seriously injured his right knee that he limped out of the game, leaving Arsenal with ten men and eventual 1-0 losers to Newcastle United. Time and again finals had been ruined by injuries and the Wembley grass had taken on a jinx reputation. "Fingers crossed," said Walley, looking into the BBC camera, "today's final is not wrecked by an injury to a player from either team."

Danny Blanchflower, Bobby Smith and Dave Mackay sat watching the live broadcast in their hotel rooms, each knowing and fearing that they could easily break down.

David Coleman asked Barnes to predict the winners. Blanchflower and Mackay openly laughed at his verdict but no doubt were concerned deep down by his answer:

QUOTE – Walley Barnes: ‘I continue to think that the Double is the impossible dream. Wing-halves Danny Blanchflower and Dave Mackay are far too occupied with attacking, and I believe Leicester will exploit the space they leave behind them. Most of the experts I know are going for Tottenham. Well I am the exception. For me this is going to be Leicester's day, provided they can avoid the injury hoodoo.’

Shortly before the final countdown came the bombshell news that Leicester had dropped their centre-forward Ken Leek, who had scored in every round. It made no sense to anybody in either camp, and it threw a huge responsibility on the shoulders of the little-known player named in his place, 20-year-old Hugh McIlmoyle. Nobody could make head-nor-tail of the decision by Leicester manager Matt Gillies, but perhaps Bill Nicholson got closest to it when he said: "They think we have been giving Leek a lot of attention in our tactical talks, but we have been concentrating more on how to break down their defence than stop their forwards."

It made even less sense when the Spurs players settled down in the hotel television room to watch the Road to Wembley films showing how each team had got to the final. Leek featured in every one of the Leicester matches, scoring goals that had got his club to Wembley. He was reported to have broken down and cried when Gillies told him he was out of the team.

The Leicester players spent Friday night at the Dorchester Hotel, where the Royal suite was taken by Elizabeth Taylor and Richard Burton.

QUOTE – Frank McLintock, Leicester's attacking right-half who was also a part-time painter and decorator: ⁶Elizabeth Taylor was stunning, and she kept staring at me in the hotel foyer. Eventually she came over to me and I thought my magnetism had drawn her to me. She said: 'I hope you don't mind my asking, but why are you wearing bicycle clips?' I had ridden my bike to catch the team coach at Filbert Street and had forgotten to take my clips off. Can you imagine that today? Frank Lampard or Steven Gerrard cycling to the ground?⁹

Leicester had taken an exhausting marathon route to Wembley. They played nine FA Cup ties in total, with replays in the fifth and sixth rounds and two replays in the semi-final. Their sixth-place finish in the First Division table was City's highest since the 1920s. The inside-forward trio of Albert Cheesbrough, Jimmy Walsh and No 9 Ken Leek had scored 50 goals between them. Their outstanding performances were a 6-0 dismantling of Manchester United, five goal beatings of West Ham and Newcastle, and home and away victories over Arsenal. And above them all was their victory over Tottenham in February when they became the first team of the season to win at White Hart Lane, two of their goals in the 3-2 win coming from Ken Leek.

That was the day that Leicester wing-halves McLintock and Colin Appleton had managed to boss the midfield, where Tottenham were used to being supreme. In goalkeeper Gordon Banks they had arguably the finest last line of defence in the land, perhaps the world. With all these facts at the fingertips, it made a bit of a nonsense for Tottenham to be such short-odds favourites. Perhaps Walley Barnes was one of the few experts who was getting his prediction right?

Leicester's long and winding road to Wembley took in a replay victory over

Maurice Norman, who was happy to discover that he would not be marking Ken Leek

Birmingham City (two goals from Leek clinching victory), a quarter-final replay win at Barnsley (an extra-time winner from Leek), and then two goalless semi-final duels with Sheffield United before goals from Walsh and Leek in the second replay booked their place against Tottenham in the final at Wembley.

Even fifty years on, nobody at Leicester can satisfactorily explain why Ken Leek was dropped, when he was considered the main goal threat to Tottenham. Their players were as perplexed as the press.

QUOTE – Frank McLintock: ⁶We players were as astonished as everybody else when Ken told us he was out. We thought he was pulling our legs until tears started rolling down his cheeks. To this day I have no idea why Matt Gillies dropped him. He said it was a tactical move and that he considered Hughie McIlmoyle more likely to be able to upset the Spurs defence. That was cobblers. When I became Leicester manager I looked back through the boardroom minutes to see if there was any reference as to why he was axed, but there was not a mention of it. There were all sorts of rumours that Ken had broken a midweek club curfew and was seen drinking in a pub. But that was never proved.⁹

Maurice 'Mighty Mo' Norman, who would have had the task of marking Leek, admitted: "I was delighted by the news. Leek was a real handful, and it made no sense at all that Leicester had decided to leave him out. I knew next to nothing about McIlmoyle, but it seemed a hell of a gamble to pitch him into such a vital match when he was so inexperienced and just twenty years old."

Both Gillies (1998) and Leek (2007) have passed on, and so their secrets have gone to the grave. The Fleet Street gossip machinery went into overdrive but nobody has ever come up with a definite reason for the axing. Perhaps it really was as simple as Gillies thinking that McIlmoyle would prove a surprise package after Spurs had spent their build-up planning to stop Leek. But it just does not ring true.

David Coleman and the BBC team of pundits spent little time discussing McIlmoyle because they knew hardly anything about him. It must have been embarrassing for Gillies to watch their hours of build-up in which they continually screened clips of Leek scoring the vital goals that got Leicester to Wembley.

As the two team coaches, accompanied by police outriders, drove through the jam-packed roads to Wembley the question on many lips was: "Why no Ken Leek?"

We will never ever know.

The 1961 FA Cup Final

May 6, 1961   Wembley Stadium   Attendance 100,000
TOTTENHAM 2, LEICESTER CITY 0

WHAT should have been one of the greatest days in British footballing history in general and Tottenham's in particular turned out to be as flat as a punctured tyre. Everything transpired to make it a match that would not live long in the memory, yet – a contradiction – it would go down in the annals as the game in which Bill Nicholson's Spurs were lifted into the land of legend.

The perfect playing weather of the Friday had been replaced by the worst sort of conditions for a flowing game. A blustery wind was trapped in the Wembley bowl, and overnight the grass had become spongy and unresponsive.

QUOTE – Danny Blanchflower: **'**If we'd had Friday's weather on Saturday we would have produced a much better spectacle. When we inspected the pitch 24 hours ahead of the game, we made up our minds that we would wear rubber studs, but we unanimously decided to switch back to our usual leather studs after we had seen the pitch an hour before the kick-off. There was rain in the air and a swirling wind that we knew was going to make ball control difficult. We were going to need all the grip we could get. I was quite concerned because, to use the old cliché, the conditions could be a great leveller. I felt we had a much stronger and more skilful all-round unit than Leicester, but the weather I realised was not going to be condusive to our style of passing game. I could not wait for the game to start to shake off this belated apprehension after months of super confidence.**'**

During the tense hour in the dressing-room leading up to the pre-match introductions, Bill Nicholson quietly sat alongside each player in turn and reminded them of their special duties that had been agreed in the White Hart Lane and Cheshunt training sessions. He asked Blanchflower and Mackay in turn if they were happy to play with their niggling injuries. They assured him they were perfectly fit, although each of them harboured private fears that they could break down.

Trainer Cecil Poynton had made a large sponge protector to wrap around Mackay's damaged shin, and the pads he chose to wear were twice as thick as usual. Blanchflower thought his knee had responded well to a week of heat treatment, but knew he dare not risk making tackles. He had long ago realised that because of physical frailities with his 34-year-old knees his role as a defender was to shepherd forwards into cul de sacs. He left the power tackles to Mackay, Norman and full-backs Baker and Henry.

Bobby Smith had kept to himself that his knee had been hurting like hell for two weeks. He was accustomed to playing through the pain barrier. Bobby was such a physical competitor that he rarely came off the pitch without bumps and bruises. He looked on playing in the FA Cup final as the greatest honour of his career, and had the painkiller injections from his doctor rather than tell Bill Nick that he was in agony.

> **QUOTE** – Bobby Smith: ⁶You have to remember that none of us were making fortunes. There was still the maximum £20 a week wage. We played for the glory, and there was no greater glory than playing at Wembley in an FA Cup final. I was not going to miss that for the world. I knew that once the whistle went I would forget all about my knee problems. I was determined to enjoy the day, and I crept out of the dressing-room twenty minutes before the kick-off to stand in the tunnel and listen to Abide With Me. It brought tears to my eyes, it was so moving.⁹

Bill Nick walked around the dressing-room shaking hands with each of his players. Danny Blanchflower made a brief speech: "We have set records all season. Now let's go out and set another, the big one ... the Double."

You could almost warm your hands on the team spirit, as the players quietly wished each other luck. Trainer Cecil Poynton, a shy man who had given his life to the club as a player and backroom servant, tried to make a Churchillian speech and choked on his words. The lads laughed. He finished up with: "Good luck you 'orrible bastards."

Final word to Bill Nick: "We have done all the hard work, now go out and enjoy yourselves. Play your natural game that has served us so well this season. Just remember what I always tell you, 'Don't come off that pitch thinking you have done less than your best.' Keep it simple, keep it fluent and let the passes flow. It does not come bigger than this ... The Double. Good luck, boys. I know and you know that you can do it. Go out there and make history."

Cliff Jones and John White cuddled each other like the brothers they felt they were.

"The atmosphere was tense yet somehow relaxed, if that makes sense," Cliff said later. "There were nerves, of course there were, but we sensed this was our destiny. Several of the lads had ciggies going. That was the way back then. A couple of the lads were sick in the loos. This was the big one. The biggest game of our lives. We had put so much into that season, we were not going to cock it up at this final stage."

As they filed out ino the tunnel leading up the long slope to the pitch, there were sincere handshakes and pleasantries as the two teams lined up alongside each other in time-honoured fashion. England team-mates Bobby Smith and Gordon Banks hugged each other, Scottish team-mates Frank McLintock and John White jokingly mimed as if to hit each other, and at the front managers Matt Gillies and Bill Nicholson wished each other an enjoyable afternoon, and then it was time for captains Danny Blanchflower and Jimmy Walsh to lead out the teams.

Moments earlier the teams had been announced over the tannoy:

Tottenham Hotspur: Brown, Baker, Henry; Blanchflower (capt.), Norman, Mackay, Jones, White, Smith, Allen, Dyson.
Leicester City: Banks, Chalmers, Norman; McLintock, King, Appleton; Riley, Walsh (capt.), McIlmoyle, Keyworth, Cheesebrough.

Following the National Anthem, Her Royal Highness the Duchess of Kent was first introduced to the Leicester players, followed by a posse of Football Assocation officials. The Duchess had a puzzled look as she walked across the red carpet to meet the Spurs players. As she shook captain Danny's hand, she asked: "Why do the Leicester players have their names on the backs of their tracksuits, yet you do not?"

"Well," said Danny, summoning up the famous Blanchflower blarney, "We all know each other."

It was a classic remark, but sadly not a classic match.

The mixture of nerves, a spongy pitch and then steady, hard rain all played a part in making it difficult for either team to get a rhythm. The Tottenham passing movements that had wrecked defences throughout the season lacked their usual accuracy and penetration. Hard as the Tottenham fans tried, they could not lift their team into revealing their true talent. The atmosphere in the ground was flat and uninspiring, mainly because half the spectators did not have allegiance to either team.

The bookmakers had made Tottenham odds-on to win, but veteran Cup followers were aware that Wolves in 1939 were even bigger favourites before going down to

The Way We Were. Here's a gathering of Tottenham fans at Wembley for the historic 1961 FA Cup final. It is an hour before the kick-off. There is not a replica club shirt in sight. And look at Wembley, not a sign of a roof and in this section they are all standing. Who is going to tell them that there is rain on the way? Their much-prized tickets cost fifteen shillings each (75p).

defeat by Portsmouth. Much had been made by the press in all the ponderings over the Double that three previous League champions had gone into the final during the century with the title wrapped up: Sunderland, Newcastle United and Manchester United. All three had gone down in the final to Aston Villa, the previous winners of the Double back in the 19th Century.

After eight undistinguished minutes there was an action replay of the John White mimed moment when he had been clowning with Cliff Jones the previous day. Mackay and Terry Dyson combined to put him clear, and the slim, pale-faced Scot clattered the ball over the bar from eight yards. He dare not look in the direction of his mate, whose prediction had come true.

It was Leicester who got the better of the opening exchanges. They were the more relaxed, playing with the air of a team determined to show the critics that they were wrong in writing them off before a ball had been kicked. McIlmoyle did not look overawed by his surprise role as replacement for Ken Leek, and he was pulling Maurice Norman out of position by deliberately playing deeper than the orthodox Leek would have done.

Frank McLintock was proving more effective in midfield than Danny Blanchflower, whose usually immaculate timing was off. A superb crossfield pass from McLintock found winger Howard Riley in space. He fired a hanging centre into the swirling wind, and McIlmoyle managed to reach it but was off-balance and directed the ball off target.

Trainer Cecil Poynton had to come on twice during the opening blitz from Leicester, first to treat Cliff Jones after he had dived into Walsh's flying boot; then to use his magic cold sponge on Peter Baker, who was knocked out when bravely throwing himself towards Cheesebrough to stop him scoring what looked a certain goal.

The game was turned on its head and destroyed as a spectacle in the 19th minute when the dreaded Wembley injury hoodoo struck yet again. Just moments after Baker had recovered from his sickening moment, his opposite number in the Leicester team – Len Chalmers – was sent tumbling by a tackle from Les Allen.

Chalmers writhed in agony right in front of the Royal Box, and it was obvious that he was seriously injured. This was the seventh time in the last nine finals that the jinx had claimed a victim, and yet again a debate started about the necessity to introduce a substitute rule. It would be another five years before the powers that be finally accepted that it made sense.

The unfortunate Chalmers was reduced to a limping passenger on the wing, and Leicester had to have an emergency shuffling of their side. McLintock – who had been having a storming game – dropped from right-half to right-back, with Ken Keyworth moving from inside-left to the McLintock role. Cheesebrough switched to the right wing, and Chalmers hobbled down the left touchline, every step obviously painful.

As so often happens, the team with only ten fit players raised their energy levels and Leicester hurried and harried every Tottenham player in possession. Bill Nicholson's well thought-out tactics were suddenly redundant, because the shape of the Leicester team had changed beyond recognition.

Skipper Blanchflower, perhaps with his mind on his ailing father, was not showing his usual composure and concentration, and was having probably his worst game of a season in which he had set sky-high standards.

Wingers Cliff Jones and Terry Dyson were both playing with great pace and desire, but they were not getting the normal support from the players inside them. Bobby Smith was bouncing off Leicester's Scottish-granite centre-half Ian King, and Les Allen had been visibly affected by his collision with Chalmers. He later admitted: "The incident ruined my game. It was a pure accident, but I felt really upset. Anybody who knows me will acknowledge that I have never ever been the sort of player who would deliberately hurt somebody."

Slowly, Tottenham began to gain the ascendancy against their handicapped opponents, and in the 37th minute they were celebrating what seemed to most people a good goal by the flying Cliff Jones, who was looking the most dangerous forward on the pitch.

Cliff went off on a celebratory run, not realising the the linesman's flag was up signalling that it was off-side. Few witnesses agreed with the linesman, but referee Jack Kelly went with him and ruled out the goal.

> **QUOTE** – Cliff Jones: •In seconds I experienced euphoria and then sudden despair. I had raced so fast that the linseman could not keep up with me, and he failed to see that Frank McLintock was playing me onside. I started to celebrate what I thought was a Wembley goal, something I had dreamed about. I could not believe it when the referee accepted the linesman's decision when he must have seen I was not off-side. To this day, I get angry thinking about it. I felt cheated out of a perfectly good goal.•

Cheesebrough darted free in the closing moments of the first-half and out of the corner of his eye he saw that there was a blue-shirted player in space. He found him with a perfect pass, and then threw his hands up in despair when he realised it was the helpless Chalmers, who could do nothing but knock the ball back into the path of Peter Baker, who with great relief kicked it clear.

Bill Nicholson brought calm to the dressing-room at half-time, telling his players they had got the bad football out of their system. "Go out in the second-half and play your natural game," he said. "I know the conditions are not in our favour but there is still no substitute for playing the sort of football that has brought us so much success this season. The Leicester players have run themselves into the ground, and you can take advantage as they begin to tire. I want concentration, I want composure and I want you to be more deliberate with your passing and shooting. There has been too much snatched stuff." He clapped his hands together. "Come on, you are just forty-five minutes away from the Double."

Skipper Blanchflower, who had been finding his form late in the first-half, said: "Let's look on the bright side. That was as bad as we've played all season, and we are still on level terms. Let's get out there and play them off the park."

Bill Nick was proved right. The Leicester players had run themselves to the edge of exhaustion, and Tottenham started to stitch together the sort of flowing movements that had carried to them to the League championship in such style. Dave Mackay, who had been operating at a lot less than normal power, began to dominate the left side of midfield, and set up a series of probing raids with his beauifully weighted left-footed passes.

The soaking Wembley pitch was dragging on the legs of the overworked Leicester team, and their gallant defence was finally pierced in the 69th minute. The long-awaited breakthrough came following one of those length-of-the-field movements that Tottenham fans had got to know so well. Ron Henry, playing to his absolute peak, dispossessed Cheesebrough deep in the Tottenham half, and the ball moved on a stream of passes through White, Smith, Jones, Dyson and Allen, who knocked it back to Dyson on the right. He moved towards the centre before firing the ball through the heart of the Leicester defence to the feet of Bobby Smith. He brought the ball under control and all in one movement swivelled round the close-marking King and beat the diving Gordon Banks with a power-packed shot from twelve yards.

It's amazing the effect a goal can have. Suddenly Tottenham were pushing the ball about with all the confidence and precision they had shown on their way to Wembley, while the Leicester players looked as if they'd had all the energy sucked out of them.

How sad for Leicester that Len Chalmers, the player who had heroically insisted on staying on the pitch when most would have surrendered to the pain, was reluctantly involved in the Double-clinching goal in the 77th minute.

Struggling on his one good leg, he failed to control the ball and it ran free – ironically – to the feet of Allen, who had accidentally been reponsible for the Chalmers injury. He transferred it to Bobby Smith, who exchanged passes with John White before racing down the wing and then sending over a pin-pointed centre. It found Terry Dyson unmarked in the six-yard box, and he headed one of the most memorable goals of his life (Smith crosses to Dyson ... goal! It was usually the other way around).

Tiny Terry set off on his trademark Indian war dance celebration run. The ever-sporting Leicester half-back Colin Appleton shouted, "Well done, Terry" as he raced past,

Skipper Danny Blanchflower is chaired and cheered after Spurs have clinched the Double at Wembley

with Dyson's team-mates trying to catch up with him to add their congratulations.

That was it. Done and dusted. There was no way back for Leicester. They had given it their all. For at least half the game they had looked the side more likely to win against a history-making Tottenham team that never quite found the form that had taken them into the annals of sporting history as the first side since Aston Villa in 1897 to win the League Championship and FA Cup.

QUOTE – Frank McLintock: 'I was so choked that I threw my runners-up medal in disgust. Thankfully, a team-mate picked it up and slipped it into my pocket in the dressing-room. We honestly felt we could win, and might have done but for the injury to Len Chalmers. But I do not want to take anything away from Tottenham. For most of the season they had looked one of the all-time great sides. Their football was a thing of beauty. Ten years later I was captain of the Arsenal team that won the Double. We did not wrap it up until the last five days of the season, clinching the title on the Monday before the final at, of all places, White Hart Lane. That was memorable for us, but it is the Spurs Double team that have got a permanent place in history. They were the first do to it in modern times. I felt privileged to play against them.'

As the players waited to take the famous 39 steps up to the Royal Box to collect the Cup and their medals, Bill Nicholson shook hands with each of them in turn, spending most time congratulating Ron Henry. They had played together many years earlier, and Ron had just produced one of the greatest performances of his career. Along with Cliff Jones, he had been the pick of the Tottenham players.

There was acknowledgement for Terry Medwin from each of the Spurs players as they went past him on the way up the steps. He had played a huge part in the season, and nobody at the club would forget it. This was very much a squad success.

Bill Nicholson seemed the least emotional of all the people in the ground as Blanchflower received the Cup from the Duchess of Kent. The dourest of dour Yorkshiremen, he admitted that jumping about was not his style. Deep down he was disappointed that Tottenham had not finished off with the style and sophistication that had marked many of the team's performances that season. Bill was a perfectionist from the top of his head to the tip of his toe, and he always wanted things just right.

Dave Mackay also felt flat in victory. "The Chalmers injury robbed the game of

Illustrator Art Turner captures the triumphant Tottenham team on their lap of honour around Wembley with the FA Cup, and that's goalscoring hero Terry Dyson being crowned with the trophy by skipper Danny Blanchflower and the other goalman Bobby Smith.

its rhythm, not only for Leicester but also for us," he said. "People will always be wondering if we would have won against eleven fit players. It's all a bit of an anti-climax."

After collecting the trophy Danny was able to say to the distinguished old gentleman standing to the Duchess of Kent's right: "I told you so." It was the veteran club chairman Fred Bearman with whom Danny had first shared thoughts of the Double in the summer of 1960.

The Leicester players formed a corridor of honour for the Tottenham players and applauded their achievement with a sportsmanship that brought tears to the eyes of onlookers in the days when football was still very much a sport rather than big business.

> **QUOTE** – Gordon Banks: ⁶We were gutted that we had lost, and it might so easily have been a different story but for the injury to Len Chalmers. Until he got his knock we were definitely the better side. But let's not take anything away from Tottenham. They had created history, and for much of the season had been the best team in the country by miles. It was truly a privilege to play against them and when we formed our guard of honour at the end it was a sincere recognition of their magnificent achievement in completing the Double.⁹

This was all fifty years ago. For the lucky few, it lives on in the memory bank as if it was yesterday,

Tottenham Hotspur, winners of the League Championship and FA Cup.

The Double had been achieved for the first time in the 20th Century.

Yes, they had provided poetry in motion ...

Brown, Baker, Henry
They roll off the tongue like old friends
Blanchflower, Norman, Mackay
Creating a legend that never ends
Jones, White, Smith
They played the game with style and flair
Allen, Dyson, Medwin
And were – at the double – beyond compare

Bill Nicholson: This WAS His Life

Norman Giller books Mr Tottenham

DURING my fourteen years as a member of the *This Is Your Life* scriptwriting team, I was continually trying to get Bill Nicholson booked. One of my roles was to prepare dossiers for the show's producer, Malcolm Morris, who would run them past Eamonn Andrews and, for the later series, Michael Aspel.

Sadly, a much deserved tribute never got past the programme planning stage. But at least this book – dedicated to the memory of Bill Nicholson and his captain, Danny Blanchflower – gives me the chance to take a microscope to Bill's life and times.

One of the reasons they were nervous about featuring Bill was that his close confidante Blanchflower had famously turned down Eamonn and told him politely where to stick his red book. It cost thousands to scrap the planned show, because relatives, clubmates and friends had been brought from all parts of the globe to join in a tribute to Danny Boy that never ever took place. The fear was that Bill – a shy, private man – might be tempted to "do a Danny."

I was privileged to get friendship-close to Bill Nick during my Fleet Street reporting career for the *Daily Herald* and *Daily Express*, so I knew him better than most. Bill was one of the few managers who used to work every Sunday, going to White Hart Lane from his nearby terraced house to catch up on the paperwork that he hated. He was very much a tracksuit manager, and only really content when at the Cheshunt training ground working on tactics and theories with his 'other family' – the players.

Virtually every other Sunday during the football season my best pal Harry Miller, of the *Daily Mirror*, and I would drop in on Bill at his cramped little White Hart Lane office. It would always start off with him moaning at us for interrupting his letter answering chores. "Here they are, bloody Miller and Giller Songs-At-The-Piano again," he would say, but then once he relaxed we would not be able to switch him off as he talked football matters. We rarely got stories for our papers because Bill did not go in for the sort of gossip editors were interested in, but it was so fascinating to hear him giving his thoughts on the game that we used to almost sit in awe at his feet.

Bill Nicholson with the Double-winning team of his dreams. Back row, left to right: Bill Brown, Peter Baker, Ron Henry, Danny Blanchflower (captain), Maurice Norman, Dave Mackay, Bill Nick; front: Cliff Jones, John White, Bobby Smith, Les Allen, Terry Dyson.

I have fished out the dossier I compiled for the eyes of Eamonn Andrews in 1985, and here it is in the original note form (the quotes were put in to give Eamonn a taste of what the guests might say). We had to give each proposed subject a codeword because if ever it leaked out that a *Life* show was being planned it would be instantly shelved. Here, published for the first time for this Golden anniversary of the Double, are my confidential notes:

TIYL BILL NICHOLSON DOSSIER
Suggested codeword: Cockerel

Summary: William Edward Nicholson, footballer and football manager: born Scarborough, Yorkshire, 26 January 1919; played for Tottenham Hotspur 1936-55, manager 1958-74, managerial consultant West Ham 1975-76; currently managerial consultant at White Hart Lane; capped once for England 1951; OBE 1975.

Personal: Married to Grace (known as Darkie). They have two daughters, and throughout his managerial career with Tottenham lived in an end of terrace house within walking distance of the White Hart Lane ground.

Quote (circa 1970) from Darkie, a down-to-earth and bubbling lady: "I accept that Bill has two marriages – one to me, the other to football in general and Tottenham Hotspur in particular. Even when we are on summer holiday in Scarborough his mind is eaten up with ideas for the following season. Sometimes I wonder if he should have a bed put in his office at White Hart Lane!"

EARLY LIFE: Born and raised between the wars in Scarborough, the second youngest of a hansom-cab driver's nine children. Grew up during the Depression, and on leaving school at the age of 14, he took a job as a laundry boy and played his football for Scarborough Young Liberals and Scarborough Working Men's Club – holding his own against grown men. In 1936, aged 16, he was spotted by Spurs and moved south to join their nursery club, Gravesend and Northfleet, before turning professional in 1938. Best person to cover this part of his footballing life is Ronnie Burgess, who captained Spurs and Wales in the 1950s and was Bill's close pal.

Quote (circa 1961) from Ron Burgess: "Bill was the most conscientious footballer I ever played with. He gave 100 per cent in everything that he did, and would always put the team first. In those early days at Gravesend and then in the first-team he unselfishly agreed to play at left-back, even though he was essentially right-footed. He lost his best years to the war, otherwise he would have won a load of England caps."

WAR YEARS: Bill had just started to establish himself in the first-team when war was declared in September 1939. He served in the Durham Light Infantry, stationed mainly in England – first as an infantry instructor, then a physical training instructor – and found time for Saturday wartime League guest appearances with Middlesbrough, Sunderland, Newcastle United and Darlington. When he reported back to Tottenham in 1945 he first of all played at centre-half and then switched to right-half, the position in which he was to establish himself as one of the most reliable and industrious players in the League. He became a key man in the Tottenham 'Push and Run' team that in back-to-back seasons 1949 to 1951 won the Second Division and First Division titles.

An imaginative view of the Double team provided by legendary Daily Mirror *photographer Monte Fresco.*

Note to Eamonn: Ideally we should bring in Alf Ramsey here, but he always refuses to do the show. I think he is in fear that he will be the subject, and likes to keep his gypsy background private. Instead, we can go for Eddie Baily, who was the schemer in that Push and Run team...

Quote (circa 1967) from Eddie Baily, England and Tottenham inside-left and later coach, who was nicknamed the Cheeky Chappie after comedian Max Miller: "Bill was a players' player. He did not hunt personal glory but gave everything he had to the team. You could count his bad games on the fingers of One Arm Lou (a notorious ticket spiv of the time). The Push and Run side would not have functioned nearly so well without Billy's energy and enthusiasm. He covered for Alf behind him and prompted the forwards with neat rather than spectacular passes. He left those to me! He learned a lot from our great manager Arthur Rowe, and when he retired it was obvious he would make an outstanding coach and manager. He was a born tactician."

PLAYING CAREER: Bill played 314 League games for Spurs as a defensive midfield player, and scored six goals. He won one England cap for England as stand-in for injured Billy Wright – against Portugal at Goodison Park in May 1951 when he was 32. Remarkably, he scored with his first kick in international football, hitting the net from 20 yards with a first-time drive in the first minute. He never got another call-up because of the consistency of Billy Wright.

Quote (circa 1980) from Billy Wright, England and Wolves captain, former Arsenal manager and now Head of Sport at ATV: "Typical of Bill, when I told him he had deserved another chance with England he said, 'No, you're the better player and the No 4 England shirt belongs to you.' I have rarely known such a modest man, and he is the perfect role model for young players coming into the game and also young managers. I may have been a better player, but it was no race as to which of us was the better manager! He was one of the top three in the game. His coaching ability was second to none."

THE COACH: In 1954, Bill was honest enough to admit that his troublesome knee would not allow him to play at full power any more and he voluntarily stood down from the team and, after helping the reserves for a while, retired to concentrate on on his first love of coaching. He gained his FA coaching badge at the first attempt and worked with the Tottenham youth squad and also with the Cambridge University team. In 1957 he became assistant to manager Jimmy Anderson, who had replaced the unwell Arthur Rowe. In 1957 he was a member of the coaching staff that travelled to Sweden for the 1958 World Cup finals.

Quote (circa 1968) from Sir Walter Winterbottom, England manager 1947-1962 and later chairman of the Central Council for Physical Recreation: "I assigned Bill to watch the Brazilians durng the 1958 games in readiness for our match. He came back with his head full of tactical plans, and we sat down and worked out how we could stop a team that was beating everybody in sight. It was largely due to Bill's creative input that we held Brazil to a goalless draw. It was an extraordinary performance against a team that became arguably the greatest world champions ever. Bill has proved beyond question that he is one of the most astute managers and coaches our game has ever produced."

Bill juggled his Tottenham manager's role with taking charge of the England Under-23 summer tours for many years, and was the choice of a lot of good judges to take over the England job before his old Tottenham team-mate Alf Ramsey was made manager in 1962.

THE CLUB MANAGER: In October 1958, Bill was appointed manager in place of Jimmy Anderson and on the very day that he took charge Spurs beat Everton 10-4! The star of the match was 'Tom Thumb' Tommy Harmer, who scored one goal and helped created seven others ...

Quote (circa 1980) from Tommy Harmer, Tottenham's tiny tot midfield schemer and now a messenger in the City: "It was one of those matches when everything we touched turned to goals. When we came off at the end I said to Bill, 'Don't expect this every week, Boss.'"

The greatest feat with which Bill will always be associated was the League and FA Cup Double of 1960-61, the first time it had been achieved in the 20th Century and considered the 'Impossible Dream.' Bill and his captain Danny Blanchflower were the driving force that lifted Tottenham into the land of legend. Many experts rate that Double team the greatest British club side of all time.

Note to Eamonn: The perfect person to produce here would be Danny, but after your previous experience I am sure you will not second that opinion! So I suggest Dave Mackay, the heart of the Spurs...

Quote (circa 1984) from Dave Mackay: "Bill was a master tactician, who could see a game in his mind before it was played. He had a photographic memory when it came to footballers, and could recall instantly the strengths and weaknesses of almost any player he had ever seen. I considered myself fortunate to play under him and tried to take his attitude and application into management."

The summer after completing the Double, Bill went to Italy and bought Jimmy Greaves from AC Milan for £99,999 (not wanting to give Jimmy the pressure of being the first £100,000 footballer). That following season Spurs won the FA Cup and reached the semi-finals of the European Cup, going out in controversial circumstances to eventual champions Benfica. This should be when we spring Jimmy Greaves (with whom I am currently writing our sixth book together):

Quote (circa 1985) from Jimmy Greaves: "Bill would not be my choice as company for a night out on the town, but he would be first on my list of managers. He can be dour and tunnel visioned where football is concerned, but he does not see his job to be a comedian. His teams always entertain on the pitch, and that's because he gives them free rein. He never tried to put any restrictions on me and I enjoyed the freedom. We won the FA Cup for Bill in 1962, which was consolation for not beating Benfica in the European Cup semi-final. I had a perfectly good goal ruled off-side, which would have given us a chance of reaching the final."

The following season Tottenham created history by becoming the first team to win a major European trophy, with a 5-1 victory over Atletico Madrid in the European Cup-Winners' Cup final in Rotterdam. We could have fun here by bringing on Bill's big pal Bill Shankly...

Quote (circa 1973) from Bill Shankly, legendary Liverpool manager: "Bill is the canniest manager in the business, who always comes up with tactical thoughts that make the difference between winning and losing. He showed us all the way to win in Europe, and has set standards that we are all trying to match. I have enormous respect for him as a manager and as a man."

In less than a year Nicholson lost the engine room of his dream team. Skipper Danny Blanchflower retired with a knee injury, the swashbuckling Dave Mackay suffered a twice-broken leg, and John White was tragically killed when struck by lightning on a golf course. Bill set about rebuilding his side and brought in Pat Jennings from Watford, Cyril Knowles from Middlesbrough, Alan Mullery from Fulham, Mike England from Blackburn, Alan Gilzean from Dundee and Terry Venables from Chelsea.

Quote (circa 1984) from Terry Venables: "It was close to an impossible job to follow in the footsteps of that great Double side. That is the sort of team that comes along only once in a lifetime. But we did our best and managed to win the FA Cup in 1967. Bill set the benchmarks for all future Tottenham managers."

There were victories in the the League Cup (1971 and 1973) and the Uefa Cup (1972), but Nicholson set his targets high and – disillusioned by the pay demands of several of his players and hooliganism among a section of the supporters – he resigned in 1974, but was coaxed back in a consultancy capacity by manager Steve Burkinshaw after a brief interlude at West Ham.

He was rewarded with an OBE for his services to football, while most in the game and certainly the Tottenham supporters feel he should have been given a knighthood.

As a surprise guest at the end of the show I suggest we spring Arthur Rowe, manager of the Push and Run Spurs who was a huge influence on Bill both as a player and as a coach. Bill will be thrilled to see him.

That is the end of my dossier. It was football, football, football all the way, and Bill won lasting respect and admiration for the dignified and creative way in which he represented the Beautiful Game. He thoroughly deserved the accolade of being presented with the Big Red Book.

This *was* Bill Nicholson's life. The Cockerel has landed.

Danny Blanchflower Revisited

Norman Giller remembers an old team-mate

DANNY BLANCHFLOWER and I were team-mates with *Express* newspapers in the days when I was chief football reporter for the *Daily* and Danny the thought-provoking columnist for the *Sunday*. We remained good pals after I had tunnelled my way out of Fleet Street to become an author (pretentious, moi?) and a freelance television scriptwriter and newspaper contributor.

One of my roles was *The Judge* of *The Sun*, answering readers' questions and settling pub arguments. One day I received a question that read: "If the job offer came along, would Danny Blanchflower consider returning to football as manager of Spurs?"

Danny, who could be witty, wise and weird in equal measure and all within one thought process, prided himself on never ducking a question, but on this occasion he was unusually prickly.

"All right, what do you know?" he said. "I'm sworn to secrecy."

Purely by coincidence I had stumbled on a developing story of major proportions.

"This is a genuine question from a reader," I told him. "What's going on?"

There was a long silence, which was a rare thing when talking to Danny because he liked to fill every waking moment with original ideas and unique observations. To wind him up, I used to call him Danny Blarneyflower.

"I don't want to tell you on the telephone," he said, mysteriously. "Meet me at the Alex Forbes café in half an hour."

This was a coffee house near Blackfriars' Station, a short walk from Fleet Street. It was years since it had been owned by former Arsenal star Alex Forbes but was still known to football journos by his name. It was the sort of nondescript place where you could melt into the background while meeting contacts.

There was a touch of a Len Deighton spy thriller about Danny's entrance into the coffee house. He was looking around furtively as if making sure he had not been followed. "What's with all the cloak and dagger stuff?" I asked.

Danny was obviously agonizing. "I'm going to have to ask you to give me your word

The changing of the guard: Danny Blanchflower meets Push and Run 'General' Alf Ramsey on the day he arrived at The Lane in 1954. The Double seeds were about to be sown.

that all I am about to tell you is confidential," he said. "You're going to be desperate to break the story, but because I cannot tell a lie I am going to take you into my confidence. If it leaks, it could stop me getting a job I have always dreamed about – manager of Spurs."

I spluttered into my coffee cup. "You've known me long enough to realise you can trust me," I said. "Thank goodness I'm not a staff reporter any more. My duty then would be to the newspaper."

"And then I wouldn't be telling you," said Danny, with his usual good sense. "The fact is that Bill Nick is on the point of resigning from Spurs, and he wants to put my name forward as his successor."

The newspaperman in me was aching to get that sensational story into print, but Danny had tied me into a straitjacket of secrecy.

"When you rang me and asked that question as The Judge, I thought it was your crafty way of saying you were on to the story," he explained. "Bill confided in me a week ago what he was planning, and I have been trying to talk him out of it. I've never known him so low and so lacking in appetite for the game that has been his life. He is completely disillusioned with the game. He doesn't like what he sees with the galloping greed of the players, and the violence on the terraces has sickened him. I said that perhaps he was trying to pass me a poisoned chalice."

It was a month before Nicholson's stunning decision to quit became public, and the veteran manager made no secret of the fact that he wanted Tottenham icon Danny Blanchflower to take over from him.

The board made a complete botch of it, and decided instead to hand the reins to Danny's fellow Irishman Terry Neill, a man with Arsenal-red blood.

"It can only end in tears," Danny told me privately. "Terry is an intelligent man with lots of bright ideas, but he has as much chance of being accepted at Tottenham as the Archbishop of Canterbury has of being installed at the Vatican."

It's history, of course, that Danny did eventually come back into football – as manager of Chelsea; which made as much sense as Terry Neill being appointed boss at White Hart Lane.

It was a total disaster that could be measured on the Richter Scale. Chelsea won only five of 32 matches on their way to relegation in 1978-79, and a completely humiliated Blanchflower was shown the door after just nine months in charge. Truly, a Bridge too far.

I interviewed Danny in happier times in 1971, getting him to compare the Tottenham Double-winning side with the Arsenal team that completed the League and FA Cup double exactly ten years after Danny had led Spurs to the historic "couple."

These were his considered man-by man-ratings:

GOALKEEPER, Bill Brown v Bob Wilson: "Not a lot to choose between them. Bill used to give me grey hairs with some of his positioning, but he had a good safe pair of hands and never let the side down. Wilson has made enormous improvement, and is now just a fingertip ahead of Bill in all-round goalkeeper skills. So I select Bob, but he is not in the same class as Pat Jennings."

RIGHT-BACK, Peter Baker v Pat Rice: "I often felt guilty about taking my wages because Peter did so much covering behind me. I had a dodgy knee in my last three seasons at Tottenham, and I would not have been nearly as effective without Peter working so hard. Pat is a good, solid and reliable right-back but my conscience insists I give the nod to Peter."

LEFT-BACK, Bob McNab v Ron Henry: "Ron was greatly under-estimated, and deserved more than his solitary cap for England. He had good ball control, and could tackle with venom. Bob McNab is a tigerish player who uses the ball intelligently, and just edges out Ron in my opinion."

RIGHT-HALF, Danny Blanchflower v Peter Storey: "As if I'm not going to select myself! With the greatest respect to Peter, he does not have my experience which meant I could dictate matches not only with my passing but with my thinking. It strikes me that Peter is played mainly in a destructive role. He does it efficiently but it is too negative for my taste."

CENTRE-HALF, Maurice Norman v Frank McLintock: "Frank and I had the captain's responsibility in common, and I think it fair to say we were both key players for our team. Of course, Frank was right-half in the Leicester team we beat to clinch the Double in the FA Cup final. He has switched to centre-half with impressive skill and determination, and − while Maurice had a distinct edge in the air − I would have to pick Frank to fill the No 5 shirt."

An artistic impression of Les Allen, father figure of a family footballing dynasty

LEFT-HALF, Dave Mackay v Peter Simpson: Sorry, but this is no race. Peter is one of the most consistent defenders in the country, but he is not in the same League as Dave Mackay. If I was picking a world eleven, Dave would be one of my first choices. He energised the team, frightened the life out of the opposition and had exceptional skill to go with his strength.

RIGHT WING, Cliff Jones v George Armstrong: We are talking world class – Cliff – against a good-quality domestic player. Cliff had the speed, the skill and the courage to take apart the tightest defence. His bravery was beyond belief and he used to make me shudder the way he would dive in where others feared to tread. George is a fine creative winger but cannot be mentioned in the same breath as the Jones boy.

INSIDE-RIGHT, John White v George Graham: Again, this is no race. John was the hidden ace in our team, making it tick with his measured passes and opening the way to goal with clever blind-side running. George has good skills and is a player of vision, but the inventive John White was a class above him.

CENTRE-FORWARD, Bobby Smith v John Radford: At his peak in that Double year, Bobby broke down the best defences in the land with his battering-ram strength and explosive finishing. He was not all raw power, but had deceptive changes of pace and excellent close control. John is a determined player with good positional sense and a deft touch in front of goal, but you ask any centre-half whom he would least like to mark out of Smith and Radford and I guarantee they would all go for the Tottenham man.

INSIDE-LEFT, Les Allen v Ray Kennedy: Les was the perfect partner for Bobby Smith in that Double season, playing with subtlety and skill that balanced Bobby's strength. He was unlucky to lose his place the following season to the one and only Jimmy Greaves (we are talking genius). Ray Kennedy is a strong, willing and promising player but has some way to go before he can be considered as effective as Allen.

LEFT WING, Terry Dyson v Charlie George: Our Mr Dependable, Terry could be counted on to run himself into the ground for the team. But going on potential and promise, I am giving Charlie George the final place. He is an outstanding proespect, and has natural finishing skills that you cannot teach.

So Danny's combined 'Doubles' team lined up like this (in 4-2-4 formation):

Bob Wilson (Arsenal)

Peter Baker (Spurs)

Frank McLintock (Arsenal)

Dave Mackay (Spurs)

Bob McNab (Arsenal)

Danny Blanchflower (Spurs)

John White (Spurs)

Cliff Jones (Spurs)

Bobby Smith (Spurs)

Les Allen (Spurs)

Charlie George (Arsenal)

I so wish there was a happy ending to this Danny Blanchflower Revisited tale, but – as Danny would say – it ended in tears. When I went to see him in 1991 for a thirtieth anniversary chat about the Double year I was devastated to find he could barely remember the name of a single player.

He was into the early stages of the Alzheimer's Disease that tragically made the last few years of his life a blank before he passed on in 1993, aged 67.

In his peak years, Danny was one of the most skilful and certainly most intelligent footballers I ever had the pleasure to watch and write about. Rest easy, Danny Boy.

WE wanted this to be YOUR book as much as ours, and invited Tottenham fans to share their memories of that golden 1960-61 season, or to pass on handed-down stories from previous generations. They poured in by the bucketload and we kick off with an in-depth view from **Leon Ruskin,** *a retired lawyer from South Tottenham. He has been a Spurs fan for more than 60 years, so he is well-qualified to discuss how the players who captured the Double honours in 1960-61 would fare in today's more sanitised and less physical game:*

THE Double in football and the Four Minute Mile in world athletics are now regularly achieved. They no longer hold a magical allure. But once they were unattainable targets, that captured the minds of the sporting public and the headlines of the media. Through the years the very greatest had sought to achieve these pinnacles, but all failed.

However, on May 6 1954, during a meet between British AAA and Oxford University at Iffley Road Track in Oxford, and with winds up to 25 miles per hour, a meagre 3,000 spectators witnessed the first of these quests being achieved. Roger Bannister ran the first Mile Race in a sub-4 minute time ... 3mins. 59.4 secs, to be exact.

This left just the Soccer Double, and the quest to create history became more frenetic. The great sides of the 50s, particularly Wolverhampton Wanderers and Manchester United were foiled, and the task appeared to all to be an impossible dream. Yet, in the close season of 1960, Billy Nicholson and Danny Blanchflower became convinced that by the end of May 1961 Tottenham Hotspur would be hailed throughout the land by achieving the Cup and League Double. Furthermore, they would win it with style and panache.

As captain Danny Blanchflower stated, "The great fallacy is that the game is first and last about winning. It's nothing of the kind. The game is about glory. It's about doing things in style, with a flourish, about going out and beating the other lot, not waiting for them to die of boredom."

Much has been written of the magnificent squad that wrote a Golden Page in British soccer's history books. Each man was a giant, but I have often pondered how these footballers would have fared in today's game. I say footballers, because I fear the iconic manager, Billy Nicholson, could not have abided the morality of today's games; the backhanders, outrageous remuneration and methods of paying it, the over-inflated egos of footballers, the amoral existences of footballers and the influence of agents and PR persons. All this would have been a betrayal of what the true values of the sport were. It was the true values that were the credo of Nicholson. It is because of his high standards, more than any of his achievements that this dour Yorkshireman should have been knighted.

The game itself has much changed in 50 years. The playing surface is now a manicured lawn. Then, save for the first few weeks of the season, it quickly became a muddy quagmire. Only the touchline retained any semblance of turf. Apart from these flanks, it was a major task for the groundsman to paint the soccer markings, the centre circle, goal and penalty areas.

The ball was made up of heavy leather segments and leather laces secured the bladder innards that inflated the ball. The effect of the rock hard and heavy ball on central defenders or attackers was to leave many with cerebral injuries in later life. Boots too were more akin to bovver boots. Heavy leather with solid toe caps. The studs were long and solid. The footwear was thus anything but streamlined. Little thought was given to facilitating players with aerodynamic and light boots or balls. One looks back with amazement that a skilled game could be played.

No one had played it with more style and flourish than Tommy Harmer, the diminutive Charmer of the midfield. He was sadly moved on from Spurs to Watford in the summer of 1960. Strictly speaking, therefore, he should not form part of my analysis. He had been a regular in our team from 1956 until 1960. Although this Tom Thumb was diminutive in stature, he was a giant in soccer genius.

I believe he would have relished the game today. His only shortcoming (if you will pardon the pun) was that, at times, he was not at his best in the muddy conditions. However, Danny Blanchflower insisted, after Harmer had excelled on a slow thawing frost surface, "Tottenham's diminutive Cockney genius has given performances laced with cheeky skill, proving that his subtle magic is highly potent whatever the state of the pitch."

Indeed Blanchflower described the brilliance of the man as follows: "He is quick-witted. Like the bullfighter, he mesmerises his opponent. Moving with graceful rhythm he takes the ball with perfect control impudently to the bewildered enemy; and continues past him with leisurely ease." Most of all he relished the brutish tackler as a challenge. His conjuring of the ball would leave his opponent on his backside, looking foolish. Tommy would have waxed lyrical on today's pitches with today's ball and boots.

The main heart, soul and brains of the Double squad came from our wing halves.

Tommy 'The Charmer' Harmer, who moved to Watford during the Double season.

The eloquent captain, Danny Blanchflower, was as fine a reader of the game as there has been, and an exquisite distributor of the ball. His soccer savvy, and high intellect enabled him to make tactical (if sometimes controversial) decisions on the pitch. I believe that without his high intellect to psychologically equip the team for this seemingly impossible task, the Double would not have been achieved. In those days the manager did not hog the touchline, as some are wont to do today. This gave Blanchflower some freedom, although he was occasionally called to task for major on field changes. Today, he would be driven to despair by touchline interference. Furthermore, his lack of speed and inadequate tackling ability would have been a big handicap in the current Premier League. I fancy he would have been better suited and a great success in La Liga.

His partner, Dave 'Braveheart' Mackay was a man for all seasons. This barrel-chested, craggy-faced Hercules, had a tackle which, Bryon Butler the journalist and BBC commentator, wrote, could "fell trees, demolish walls or break up tanks." However, he had instinctive ball skills. Jimmy Greaves said, "he had just about everything: power, skill, stamina and enthusiasm. He was the best professional I ever played alongside. When he was missing we all had to work twice as hard."

His soccer skills were underrated, and a favourite trick involved juggling an orange on each foot and then flicking it up and catching it on the back of his neck. Although his tackles were never dirty, I wonder how officials today would interpret them. Nonetheless, I believe we would be twice the team today if we had the greatest wing-half to emerge from Scotland in our side.

Our goalkeeper, Bill Brown, was a tall, and athletic Scottish international. Unfortunate to be the filling in the sandwich of our two greatest goalkeepers, Ditchburn and Jennings, he was not dissimilar to our current No 1, Gomes in being a great shot-stopper with a weakness on occasions for crosses. However, they differed in that Brown was a very placid and self-assured 'keeper who gave calmness to his defence. Elastically agile, although not a show-off, Brown had remarkably sharp reflexes; he also possessed an instinctive positional sense, which made much of his work, seem misleadingly easy, and his ability to maintain concentration was exceptional.

Brown's weakness with crosses was well-covered by Maurice Norman, the giant Norfolk centre-half. On the few rare occasions when Brown seemed uncertain, Norman would take control of the goal area and invariably head balls to safety while leaving the keeper to patrol his line.

A mop of hair atop Norman's head, made him appear taller than his 6 ft 1 inch. His burly physique were supported by enormous thighs. A confident player, he could be a dangerous surprise weapon in attack when needed, in the days when it was not customary for a centre-back to join the attack. He would have walked into our team today. Indeed this was an age when positions were more rigid. Full-backs did not overlap, and were vital defenders at a time when wingers were important attacking weapons. Our two full-backs, Peter Baker and Ron Henry (the only two indigenous players in the team) were of this ilk. Essential in defence, and indeed Baker was much under-valued as he had to cover the shortcomings in defence of Blanchflower. Furthermore, his style of play, with quick short passing was very much influenced by Arthur Rowe's "Push and Run." Full-back play is so different today, it is difficult to know how these two would have adapted.

Our three wingers, Cliff Jones and the two Terrys, Medwin and Dyson, not only were penetrating runners who provided deadly crosses, but were clinical finishers themselves. In 35 appearances (and remember this was a time before the admission of substitutes) the lightning fast, and brave Jones scored 19 goals; in 47 games Dyson netted 17 times; the tall Terry Medwin was the best crosser of the ball, and was a fine dribbler and strong in the air. Alas, he had largely lost his place after his best years in the late 1950s. In the Double year he only made 15 appearances but still scored 5 times. Throughout his Spurs career his 215 games produced 72 goals.

One can see that the goals came liberally from the wings as well as the central forwards. I have no doubt that Cliff Jones would have been a match-winner today, and that Dyson and Medwin would not have been found wanting.

John White was tragically cut off before he achieved the full greatness he was destined for. He was known as 'the Ghost' and in evaluating him Cliff Jones said, "He was like Glenn Hoddle. But he was different to Glenn in some ways. Glenn was someone who you had to bring into a game, whereas John White would bring himself into a game. If you're not in possession, get in position, that was John White. He was always available if you needed to pass to someone."

John was, in truth, impossible for opponents to play against, and for one looking so frail, he was fast, exquisitely balanced and could run for ever. In the season, he scored 13 goals in 49 matches. We never saw his full greatness, and he would be a dazzler today.

Our two strikers, Bobby Smith and Les Allen, both came from Chelsea in the 50s. 'Smudger' Smith in his early years was more adept at hitting the corner flag with his shooting. But once he got his range he was deadly, as 208 goals in 317 appearances will tell. In the Double year, he scored 33 goals in 43 games. He scored 13 goals in 15 appearances for England. One from the halfway line against Spain, I witnessed.

In the days when goalkeepers were not a protected species, Bobby was a battering-ram who loved to test the goalkeeper's resilience as early as possible in the match. He would have suffered from being denied this intimidation today, but he also had a delicate side to his play. His lay-offs and flick-ons to Jimmy Greaves (who arrived in

Study of a master – Jimmy Greaves, who took over from Les Allen

December 1961) produced more goals for Greaves than any other provider. However, I believe that with his bustling style curtailed, he would be only half the force he was, in today's game.

Almost as prolific in 1960/61 was the elegant and unselfish, Les Allen. He scored 27 goals in 49 games. His reward was to then yield his place to a certain Jimmy Greaves. Les was always a pleasure to watch, and will always be remembered for the five goals he scored in our 13-2 thumping of Crewe. However, I doubt if he would have been any more significant in the modern game.

So many of these legendary players are no longer with us. They are remembered with the greatest joy and appreciation. I have no doubt that they now grace the portals of the immortals in Heaven. Most certainly among the stars that twinkle the brightest are Billy Nick, Danny Blanchflower, Tommy Harmer, Bill Brown and John White.

THE GOOD AND BAD TIMES

DAVID SYMES, Sheffield

Tottenham winning the Double turned me into what I suppose might be considered a fair weather supporter because it was not until the year after that I began to watch and support them. I was 12 at the time and with a group of friends would board the special supporters trains that ran along the Eastern Line to Liverpool Street stopping at White Hart Lane. Ever since I have supported and in later days just 'followed' the team. This has been through both good times (generally when the year ended in a 1) and bad – it's always been entertaining (that's the Spurs style) but most of the time exasperating as well.

We would walk for about 10 minutes from the station in Tottenham to the ground and then join the queue for the juniors turnstiles. I seem to remember we paid a bob (a shilling in 'old money' or 5p) to get in. This was considerably less than the adult price so made the up-to-two-hour wait worthwhile. If we were late however we would pay the full amount as otherwise we could not be sure of standing somewhere where we would see much of the game. Once in the ground with our programme (often bought outside the ground), bags of Percy Dalton roasted peanuts – still in their shells – we would then join the rest of the crowd and try to get down to the front.

In the early years we would bring small, self-made wooden boxes to stand on to get a better view above the adults around us. Sometimes the grown ups took sufficient pity on us that we would be passed down to the front. All the way around the stands in those days was a low iron railing consisting of overlapping semi-circles painted white. We would establish our position by pushing our small arms through the gaps and holding our hands together tightly.

Many people have written about the atmosphere that existed in the old football grounds before they were all-seater and it is now something that few people will experience. When Spurs played one of the other top teams the attendance in the ground would near 'capacity', which for us small ones meant we would not be able to move independently until we got out of the ground after the match.

When the action on the pitch moved to the corners we would strain along with those around us to see what was happening out of sight. Never mind that we would not be able to see any better because everyone else was doing the same – we could not help ourselves. Goalmouth action would cause everyone to want to get nearer to the action, so we could move two or three steps down the ground because of the crowd behind pushing us there.

If we stood behind the many crash barriers every 8 to 10 steps or so dotted around the stands we might find ourselves almost being crushed as we could not move down any more. On one occasion I can remember the crush being so great on leaving the ground after the game that our feet did not touch the steps as we left. We were wedged shoulder to shoulder with grown ups and 'hitched' a free if somewhat terrifying ride down the steps. The trouble with this was on reaching the bottom and before our feet again made contact with the ground some of us would be herded to the right (and away from where we wanted to be going) while the others were herded left. The fight to regroup against the stream was very tiring.

On the way back to the station the new cheap Japanese transistor radios would blare out the strains of Sports Report, and because all teams played on the same day and at the same time we would listen out for other results. Cheers and groans would break out from the travelling hordes from time-to-time in response to what we were picking up on the radios. Those that had not managed to hear clearly would soon be informed by others who and what all the noise was about.

I well remember one of these moments; it was after a game at Upton Park against West Ham. Dave Mackay, a Spurs stalwart who had broken his leg the season before, was returning for the reserves after almost 12 months out of the game. We juniors decided to stay in the ground until much of the crowd had left. During the lull before the storm we listened to Sports Report on nearby transistor radios when it was reported that in his first game since breaking his leg Dave had been stretchered off and it was believed he had broken his leg again. Even in a half empty stadium this news led to a deep communal groan that was eerie because it was as if we had no individual freedom of thought but were just a collective herd. Such was the regard in the game for Dave that the groans came from all around the emptying stands – from Hammers as well as Spurs fans.

That communal feeling was most exaggerated on one occasion at White Hart Lane and is the memory I wanted to record here in this book. It was the first home game since another old stalwart of the Double winning team lost his place to a young upstart we had not heard of. The stalwart was the Scottish goalkeeper Bill Brown, the young upstart was Pat Jennings from Watford.

There was a lot of animosity toward Pat that day. That was until early on in the game with the ball heading clearly over the bar he jumped one-handed to catch it. For a split second the rumble of crowd noise was replaced with the beginnings of discontent – we could all see it was heading out for a goal kick so why try to stop it and

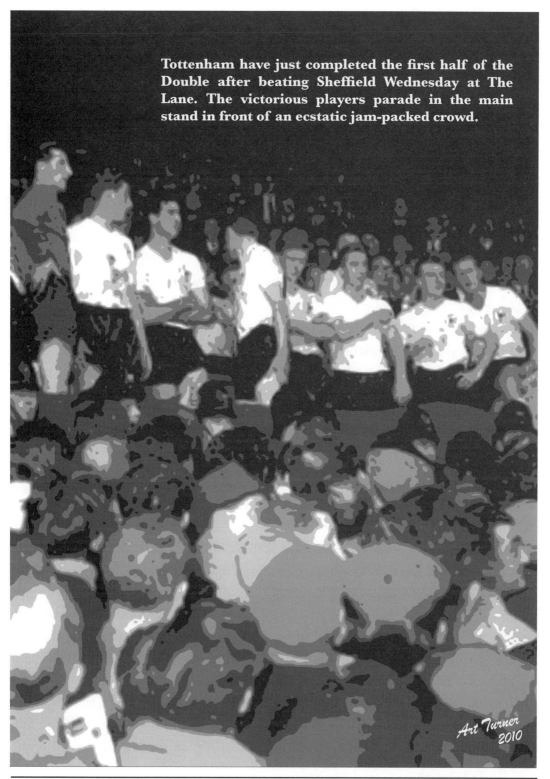

Tottenham have just completed the first half of the Double after beating Sheffield Wednesday at The Lane. The victorious players parade in the main stand in front of an ecstatic jam-packed crowd.

Art Turner
2010

perhaps give away a corner? The growing discontent was never fully voiced however because a strange thing happened that first brought the ground to a split second of utter silence (the silence of disbelief) followed by a tremendous crescendo of cheering. The young upstart had jumped one handed to stop the ball a foot or so above the bar. The ball just seemed to stick to his single glove which he curled around the ball and safely brought it down into both hands ready to thump it back into play. We could not help it – we all grumbled as one, then were all briefly silent in disbelief and finally cheered at the top of our voices to welcome a new hero.

The King is dead, long live the King. Somehow that captured the moment when the old Double heroes gave way to a new generation of Tottenham legends.

And so the ball rolls on.

WHEN SUNDERLAND HAD US IN WONDERLAND

MALCOLM PARIS, Colchester

Along with my late Dad, Marshall, I was one of the 65,000 crowd shoe-horned into the Lane for the quarter-final replay against Sunderland, which we won 5-0. There has never been a greater atmosphere, with the crowd surging on the terraces. It took an hour and a half for us to move the final few yards to get into the ground, and when I think back I realise just how dangerous it was. With all-seater stadiums, no football fan will ever experience such an exciting atmosphere again. For me, that was the outstanding game of an unforgettable season.

BILL NICK, THE JINX AND A CUPPA TEA

ALAN PRYOR, Biggleswade

My Dad, Don, who is in his seventies is a lifelong Spurs fan. He also brought me up the right way, and apart from a brief moment of madness when I was five years old (I wanted a Chelsea Bag as my first school bag, something my Mum wouldn't allow because my Dad would have hit the roof!!), I have supported Spurs for forty years. The Double side has always been special to my Dad. He has a framed photo on the wall in his house of that great side and Bill Nick was a hero to him. Unfortunately when it comes to watching Spurs live he has always been a bit of a jinx.

I remember as a child being taken to the Lane several times in the Seventies by my Dad and never seeing Spurs win. When I was old enough to go by myself the first match I went to we won, beating Everton 3-0 in 1981. In the Double season Spurs started the season with a fantastic run, winning the first eleven games. Guess who went to the twelfth? Spurs were at home to Manchester City, a side that finished in 13th place that season and Spurs were expected to beat them comfortably. Obviously my Dad going ruined the run and Spurs only drew 1-1.

He did go again that season and they did win, but he can't remember who they played. So the lasting memory of the Double season for my Dad is the first points dropped! It took me forty years to break the jinx. We saw Spurs beat Fulham 2-0 in 2005. Dad has been with me twice since then and Spurs have won both times. Although he never can relax, even when we are 3-0 up!

It is Dad's proud boast that he got to meet the great Bill Nicholson as well. He played for his local side Biggleswade Town in the early Sixties when they were in the Eastern Counties league. Tottenham 'A' side also played in the same league, and after being beaten 9-0 at Cheshunt the dejected Biggleswade players trooped off.

Bill Nick, who had been on the touchline, patted my Dad on the shoulder and said, "There's a cup of tea over there lad." My Dad never wanted to wash his shirt again! Biggleswade did play Spurs 'A' at White Hart Lane once, sadly my Dad missed it through injury. I told you he was jinxed.

A RATTLING GOOD TIME

MAUREEN TURNER, Chingford

My lasting memory of the 'Double' year is of my oldest brother and his friends partying when we won the Cup and the parade along Tottenham by the team. I was about seven years old and vividly remember being in the High Road by Paxton Road. We had the old heavy wooden rattles and blue and white pom poms. Lads were trying to throw streamers over the Trolley Bus cables. It was a brilliant experience, and the memory warms me to this day.

DAVE MACKAY, A HERO FOR ALL SEASONS

STUART BALL, Cambridge

I was lucky enough to meet Dave Mackay at a Newcastle away game in 2009 and I asked him to sign my shirt. He readily agreed but made the comment, "You can't know who I am, you're too young." I had the pleasure to tell him: "Every Spurs fan knows who you are. You're a legend."

I could tell he was proud to be seen in such a way by the fans. I may not have had the joy of seeing him and the Double team play but Dave and that Super side are legendary. It was such an honour to meet a true hero, and so rewarding to find that he is a real gent.

A SHOPPING TRIP TO REMEMBER
KEVIN FIELD, Lincoln

I first started to support Spurs towards the end of the 1950s following a shopping trip to Tottenham with my parents. Quite why we went there shopping has always puzzled me but in hindsight I am glad that we did, as it changed my life forever. I heard a roar as we were in the High Street and asked my dad what it was. He told me that it was a football match and Tottenham must be playing at home.

The following day I looked in the paper for the result and was puzzled by the entry Tottenham H. Other results had just a name or Rovers, United or City. My dad told me that the H stood for Hotspur and from that moment I was hooked. Each week, I would look for the result and started to press my dad to go and see a game.

In 1959 catastrophe struck! I was told that the family would be moving to the outskirts of Liverpool, which meant to me that I would never see my beloved Spurs play at White Hart Lane.

I remember going to the village primary school and being asked if I supported Everton or Liverpool. I replied Spurs, which brought about howls of laughter. Not only was I the new boy who spoke funny, but I supported a football team that was from London with a funny name. How I hated my time then.

Things began to change in the summer of 1960. Not only was it my 11-plus year, but my beloved Spurs started to win. Not the odd game but game after game! I clearly remember going into school and proudly telling the others that 'we won again.' This seemed to go on and on until I had to slink in as we had lost against Sheffield Wednesday. Another team with a funny name! At least I had nearly two months of being able to say we had won.

The other boys started to take an interest in the results, as they had never seen their teams win so many games. Even a classmate called Susan, whose family had Harry Catterick, the manager at that time of Everton, stopping with them, was interested. I cut out as many newspaper articles as I could get my hands on and stuck them in a scrapbook, now sadly lost.

As the season went on, I got more and more excited. I only saw the odd television report, as the coverage was nothing like it is today. I went into school on a Thursday morning in April 1961, with a grin as wide as a Cheshire Cat, after we won the League the previous night by beating Sheffield Wednesday 2-1.

I couldn't wait for the Cup final in May when I would actually see my team for the first time play a full match. Dad thought it sad that Leicester had to play with virtually ten men, following an injury to Chalmers but nevertheless celebrated with me at the final whistle.

As in those days everyone watched the Cup final, all my friends knew who had won, and as we played in the road afterwards, each wanted to be Bobby Smith. I was always John White, as like me, he seemed so quiet. So many memories and too many years since the Championship was last won.

THE FA CUP AND THE GENERATION GAME

DONALD BARKER, Waltham Cross

I was too young to have any personal memories of the double season. However, I remember walking around Devonshire Hill Infants School proudly wearing a rosette with a tin foil FA Cup in the middle. It was bought for the 1960 FA Cup tournament, but came out again for '61! Waste not want not in those days.

My main memory of that time is when they brought the FA Cup back for the parade. A friend of the family was an old Tottenham 'character' called Billy Mudge, who owned a garage and car-hire business in the High Road, just along from the ground. He was a bit of an eccentric, and always wore an old driver's peaked cap and a 'car coat' which resembled brown overalls.

Going into his office was like going into a museum, with things such as stuffed bears climbing a tree trunk, and a cross-section of a Roman drainage pipe found in the area. A visit to Billy Mudge was always a treat when I was a boy, and when Spurs won the Cup he let my family go up to the first floor and hang out the windows, which overlooked the High Road.

When the open-top bus went by, the team was on the same level as us, and passed just a few feet away, rather like the prizes on the 'Generation Game'! I guess the Cup represented the cuddly toy.

Unfortunately, my grandfather, who was a great Spurs supporter, died in 1956, and my father passed on in 1959. I have an older brother, but he went off the rails and joined the Young Conservatives instead. Could have been worse. He might have become a Young Gunner.

Not one but two trophies to show off, as the Spurs coach parades along the High Road in May 1961

BUILDING ON A STRONG FOUNDATION

STEPHEN SMITH, Kazakhstan via Essex

When Spurs beat Leicester to clinch the Double I was just a toddler, but the achievements of that season are the foundations on which so much club pride is built. By the time of the 1967 FA Cup final I was becoming more aware, and remember being given a bottle of Coca-Cola to drink as I watched Spurs win on my cousin's black-and-white TV. For me, it all took off big time with the FA Cup triumph of 1981. I was there to see Ricky's goal and we were all aware that it was 20 years since the Double and thirty years since the Push and Run days.

Bill Nick had his stars playing football just as he had learnt his trade during the Push and Run era of Arthur Rowe, gaining admiration from supporters, opposition and the press alike, playing in what was, in comparison to today's game, on poor pitches with heavy laced (god, didn't that hurt when you headed it !) balls, and not to mention the footwear. They played with style just how the game is meant to be played, and just how we Spurs fans like to see it played today. The Push and Run and Double teams provided my generation with so much to be proud about, and now Harry Redknapp is building on that foundation. I continue to watch closely from here in Kazakhstan where I am employed in the oil industry.

THE GREAT MACKAY AND THE LONG-DISTANCE THROWS

PETER HICKS, Brighton

Because I was only eight years old my memories of that Double year are quite fuzzy. My clearest memory of that season has got to be of my hero, Dave Mackay. He left a massive impression on me (as he often did on his opponents!). With his huge barrel chest stuck out, he exuded an air of invincibility. I always felt that with Dave on the pitch we couldn't lose. He was the perfect NCO to Danny's Captain. He covered vast areas of the pitch, hounding the opposition and encouraging the team. I loved it when Dave took a throw-in, so I could see him close up. My Dad began to favour the enclosure below the West Stand, where they only allowed in a certain number of spectators. Children, as I remember, paid threepence extra.

We often stood (or I was often carried because of the crowds!) near the players tunnel. Anyway, for the throw-ins, it was great to see Dave. He just arched his back, cranking himself like a medieval siege machine and sent the ball sailing into the Park Lane penalty box. To me he was, and is the complete footballer.

My memory gets better as I hit my teens, for example that wonderful match between

Spurs and the European Champions Man Utd in October 1968, 2-2. It was Cliff Jones' last game for Spurs and Gilly scored an absolute beaut! But that's another story.

Note: Peter Hicks is a distinguished author whose 'Inspirational Lives' series is in bookshops now, including close-ups on William Shakespeare, Lance Armstrong and Barack Obama. Wonder if he will ever get around to the Great Mackay?

BILL NICHOLSON SOWS THE SEEDS

BARRY HATCHER, West Byfleet

My love affair with the Spurs started in 1947 when I was 10 years old. My dad, who was born and bred in South London, had followed the Spurs since they won the FA Cup in 1921 and decided I was ready to be exposed to the wonderful world of Tottenham Hotspur FC. After a couple of seasons, Dad decided I was smitten enough to warrant buying a couple of season tickets which were the size of a credit card and priced at £3 for a season of 21 home games with Cup games extra! So we had seats for the 50-51 season which produced that wonderful style of play known as 'push and run' and the team won the Second and First Divisions in consecutive seasons. I can remember the names of the team as though they were playing today.

The goalie was Ditchburn; the full-backs Ramsey and Willis or Withers, the half-backs Nicholson, Clarke and Burgess (capt); the forward line Walters, Bennett, Duquemin, Baily and Medley – a wonderful team, with Arthur Rowe a great manager.

We continued to watch the team which sadly declined due mainly to age, but an improvement in the 1959-60 season happened when we finished third with Bill Nick now manager. The seeds for the winning double side were, in my opinion, sown when Bill Nick signed Dave Mackay from Hearts in March 1959 and Dave went on to be one of the finest players of his generation – a true giant who feared nothing.

The season started on August 20th when Spurs played Everton at home and won 2-0 but I had to miss this game as I was on honeymoon, having been married the previous Saturday.

I was back in time for the remainder of the home games and, in particular, I remember with great satisfaction Spurs beating both Man United and Arsenal before the end of September. In fact Spurs won the first 11 games and my Dad and I thought we were in for a good season!

My memories of games that were 'special' include the 4-1 victory over Man United when Bobby Smith and Les Allen each scored twice. This victory was achieved without Cliff Jones who was injured but it didn't matter as the team could have beaten any other side in the world with their unbelievable performance.

Other outstanding games were our two victories over the Arsenal – it was a great feeling pulling off the double against our close rivals.

However, the League game of the season was on December 3rd when Spurs were home to Burnley in front of over 58,000 fans. We scorched into 4-0 lead, but Burnley pulled one back just before half-time.

I had a nagging feeling we might be in trouble in the second-half and so it proved. Burnley played magnificently and scored three times to rightly earn a 4-4 draw. What a match played by two fantastic sides (Burnley proved later in the season what a great side they were by beating us 4-2).

Basically, every League game was special with the team producing a brand of football that had never been seen previously from any British team. I just couldn't believe the style we were seeing. It was breathtaking and a privilege to watch.

The First Division championship was won in a canter, especially when considering the players took it easy over the final League games to ensure they would be fit for the FA Cup final against Leicester City. Only 12 players were needed for the majority of the games, with five other players appearing in only 14 games – no subs in those days and injuries were a rarity.

With the Championship won, the team concentrated on the FA Cup and two games stand out in my memory – both against Sunderland, who were then a Second Division side. We went up to Roker Park and this is without doubt the most memorable game I ever witnessed, particularly as it ended 1-1. Spurs scored first through Cliff Jones and the first-half was ours.

I don't know what the Sunderland team had in their cup of tea at half-time but the way they came out and took control of the game was mind-blowing. The support from the home crowd was at such a volume it actually scared me and they willed on their team to equalise, which they duly did.

This equaliser increased the volume level of their support and I remember reading Danny Blanchflower saying he tried to rally the team but his words just could not be heard.

Spurs managed to hold on to earn a replay the following Wednesday. This too was a remarkable performance and it seemed the team felt they had more than a point to prove and took Sunderland apart to win 5-0. These two games were watched by over 126,000 spectators and I had been to both games – fantastic!

Spurs had to play Burnley in the semi-final at Villa Park and I can't remember anything about this match except Bobby Smith scored twice and Cliff Jones got the other goal.

So to Wembley and a final that did not produce anything really memorable except Leicester losing their right-back Len Chalmers. This final was really an anti-climax after such a wonderful season but we won 2-0 and the Double was ours – the first time this had been achieved in modern day football.

We watched Danny receive the Cup and we made our way out of the ground to where our car was parked. On the way, we passed a car which had to be owned by a Spurs fan as he had a couple of Shredded Wheat pushed onto the radio aerial. Danny was advertising Shredded Wheat in those days and I thought this was such a stylish way of showing who one supported and a perfect end to a wonderful and stylish season from the 'Team of the Century.'

TERRY DYSON, YOU LITTLE BEAUTY

COLIN ASHBY, France via Haslemere

I had started supporting Spurs when I was an eleven-year-old. My brother had introduced me to them, older than me and working in London, he had seen them play and brought the programme home for me. We lived in Dartford so it was a long way to go to see them play, the nearest team in the Football League being Charlton.

The year before we did the double was exciting and a forerunner to my expectations. We had played some good football but missed out on the championship, so when we set the record number of wins in the following season my hopes were high, however there were still the bogey teams, Burnley, Leicester, Cardiff, who could dash my hopes. I didn't mind us playing the Arsenal, Wolves or even Everton as we seemed to match them but it was these other teams, Burnley in particular always seemed to do well against us and even in the double season drew with us 4-4 and scored four to beat us at home.

I was working for Olivetti in London and remember particularly the game against Birmingham. I bought a ticket and got in at the Paxton Lane End. I was not very big and the crowded terraces made me feel like a sardine packed in, there were times as I jostled my way to be as close to the front as possible, that my feet were hardly touching the ground. We had lost our first game the week before against Wednesday so I was curious how the team would react. I recall some guy standing near me he kept on moaning about White, Dyson and Smith and when I rounded on him to have a go and saw how big he was decided discretion was the better part of valour. White I thought was outstanding in that game, such a gifted player and when he scored the opener I turned and half cheered and jeered at his detractor. Strange then we would cheer and wave our arms if we scored, years later I would hug the stranger next to me. We were quite restrained in the 60's. 6 goals that game - brilliant and we were back on track.

I could not go to the final so got myself ready to watch on telly. The whole thing – the build up before the game and then the singing, I could not sing some of them as I was too choked up with emotion and anticipation. I did not want to hope too much, others had tried and failed to do the double. We had beaten Burnley convincingly in the semi-final but we were now playing bloody Leicester, the team who had beaten us at home in February. I recall we had virtually tied up the title early so we were able to concentrate on the cup, but I felt too many results had gone against us for my liking, so although I hoped and prayed we would be the first to do the double in the century, the omens were stacked against us.

The game was not good and I felt the voodoo of champions falling at the final hurdle was going to hit us again. I sat in my living room, on my own cursing bloody Leicester.. Blanchflower was off the pace and was disappointing but so too were quite a few of the team. I have to admit I gave a bit of a cheer when one of their players was injured and became a passenger, I would take anything to help us win, but even with him just making up the numbers they were still creating chances and I have to admit looked the better side. They were no pushovers and had finished sixth in the league and thrashed Manchester United so they had something about them.

Then we scored, it was Jones. I leapt up and danced around the room, but it was disallowed for offside. "Of course it wasn't you stupid ******". We missed some opportunities to go ahead as well, but we were still not playing the fluent flowing football that had won us the league. Then deep into the second-half big burly lovable Bobby scored. It was the best goal ever as far as I was concerned, no whistle blown for offside this time, it was a goal. I danced, I cheered and then just as suddenly calmed down as there was still enough time for them to get back into the game and the tension started again. We were playing better now, a bit more like the team that had just won the league, then little Terry Dyson got on the end of a cross and headed the ball home. 2-0 ! You little beauty!

The rest of the game is now a bit of a blur, the relief when the final whistle went. We had done it!! I sat quite still in the chair, emotion and euphoria mixing and the tears started as the team led by Danny boy went up to collect the trophy and their medals. I stopped weeping as they did their lap of honour, I am convinced we were the first

Bobby Smith (centre) leads the Spurs swingalong at the FA Cup final celebration banquet at the Savoy Hotel in London, with Terry Dyson clapping along as bespectacled club assistant secretary Alan Leather plays the piano.

to start this tradition, my face was fixed in a grin of happiness and did not go for a few days. I read all the papers the following day and on the Monday, so what they had been hampered by one of their team being injured? That's football.

SPURS – TOTTENHAM HOTSPUR – had become the first team in the 20th Century to complete the elusive double. No one was going to take that away from them ... or from me.

'SIR' BILL NICK, SIMPLY THE BEST

DON MAHONEY, Potters Bar

I was not born when Spurs were winning the Double, but listening to people who were there talk of that team makes the hairs on the back of my neck stand up. I recently watched a TV show about the greatest ever managers, and to be honest it was a great top 20. They had Stein, Shankly, Revie, Busby, Paisley, Clough and Joe Mercer (when he was in partnership with Malcolm Allison at Man City). The top two were Fergie and Wenger. But I wanted to know who the public thought was the greatest manager out of the greatest managers, and I was so pleased that in the public vote 'Sir' Billy Nick beat the lot of them.

Former Arsenal and Scotland goalkeeper Bob Wilson still, to this day, ranks our Double winning team as the closest thing to football perfection he has ever seen. Praise indeed coming from a Gooner who was in the Arsenal double-winning team of 1970-71. They scrambled it, coming through late in the season and clinching the title at Tottenham of all places on the Monday and then beating Liverpool to lift the FA Cup on the Saturday.

I also had a conversation with a chap from Liverpool, who was around in the 1960s, and when I asked him about the Tottenham team it was like he had been asked the perfect question before he died so he could drift away peacefully knowing he had gone with the happiest thoughts imaginable! He closed his eyes as the birth of a huge smile grew on his face, nestled back into his chair nodding; he didn't say a word, just sat there with a huge grin and nodding away. I didn't need to ask anything else. Without saying a word, he made what I thought was a hard question damn easy.

THE BEST BRITISH CLUB SIDE EVER?

ANDY THFC WRIGHT, Andover, Hants

While growing up and following the mighty Spurs, there are two words I remember hearing more often than any others, and those words were THE DOUBLE. I started supporting Spurs from the age of 14 and regardless of how the team was performing at the time, THE DOUBLE was always mentioned and talked about on a regular basis. And so it should be. Sadly I didn't get to witness the Spurs team of the early 1960s, but having seen a lot of footage of those years and read many articles, I feel I can understand and appreciate just what a great team we had then.

I've heard many people over the years saying that the Double winning team of 1960-61 was the best British club side ever. Of course that's open to debate, but I think it's probably not far from the truth. And it got even better the following season when seeing Greavsie gliding past defenders as if they weren't there must have been a privilege for all the spectators.

Supporting Spurs today is a mixture of highs and lows, as it has been for quite a while now, but THE DOUBLE winning team of 1960-1961 only ever seemed to have high points virtually every time they went out on to the pitch. If we ever get a Spurs team anywhere near as good as that again then we really will be blessed.

COACHED BY A DOUBLE WINNING LEGEND

JAY GLOVER, Liverpool

My favourite/only link with the Double winning season was when a short ginger northerner came to teach PE at my school (approx 90-91) with a face strangely familiar to me, a die-hard Yid. Imagine my utter joy when he introduced himself as Mr Dyson. Yes, it was THE Double-winning Terry Dyson, who taught me how to play football for two years at school, and was only too happy to talk to me about everything relating to that glorious season in our history. The man was an absolute legend!

IN THE SWIM WITH THE GREAT MACKAY

STUART HYDE, Enfield

When I was a boy my family lived in Enfield, just off the Cambridge Road in Severn Drive. It was on the opposite side from the Crematorium. I used to go swimming with my mate Victor at the Enfield swimming baths – the water wasn't heated and it was bloody freezing! On one particular summer's day we were there and there were a group of people sitting by the pool and a couple of them were kicking a football. They seemed quite good, we thought, so we moved closer for a better look.

"Blimey!" I said, "That's Dave Mackay!" Dave Mackay was my football hero of the Double team. I played for the school team at left-back and tried to model myself on him – his fierce tackling – make sure you get the ball and the player! I can remember trying to stick my chest out in just the same way he did whenever I played. Anyway, I managed to find an old cigarette packet lying on the floor and quivering, bravely asked this football god for his autograph which he wrote on the back. Unfortunately it has long since disappeared in the mists of time. For me Dave Mackay epitomised what the great Spurs Double side was all about: brave, courageous, skilful, inspirational and intelligent.

Within a few years of course the double-winning team began to break up. There have only been two public figures whose deaths have shocked me – President John F. Kennedy and the second, John White – the Ghost of White Hart Lane. I can still remember standing, in stunned silence, on the grass verge on the opposite side of the Crematorium watching the funeral cortege pass by.

I will always be grateful to my father for taking me to see the Double side – a team which demonstrated everything good about the game. Like many people I can still quote that team in order – Brown, Baker, Henry, etc. I believe that team was actually improved, if that were possible, when Bill Nick managed to sign Jimmy Greaves. I have many happy memories of watching Jimmy G and the Spurs play. His hat-trick against Blackpool on his debut was brilliant. I was very saddened when I heard of Jim's battle with alcoholism and very happy for him when he got his life back on track.

I cherish the memories I have of standing on a box (which my Dad made for me) on the terraces with my Dad cheering him on. Jimmy Greaves was my boyhood hero. He still is and he is simply the greatest goalscorer ever.

Picture this: fifty seven thousand supporters, White Hart Lane. Spurs v Manchester United, Saturday October 16th 1965. In the United team – Best, Law, Charlton, Crerand, Foulkes, Stiles. In the Spurs team – Mullery, Robertson, Smith, Mackay Norman, Knowles, Gilzean and the brilliant Jimmy Greaves.

I had seen Jimmy make his debut against Blackpool when he scored a hat-trick. I saw him play against Benfica in the European Cup semi-final in 1962. I saw him play in many games but in the Spurs v United match he scored one of his greatest goals which I will never forget.

Every forward scored for Spurs that day: Alan Gilzean from a header on the back post, the second by Neil Johnson from a sublime Greavsie pass. Then came the best goal of the game. Jimmy received the ball midway inside the United half, facing towards his own goal. He spun and with lightning feet left two United players for dead. He accelerated past another and then another, pushed the ball past the goalkeeper Pat Dunne and passed the ball into the net. Superb, breathtaking and never to be forgotten. I still have the programme for that match, which Jimmy very kindly signed for me when I met him in his dressing-room at the Brewhouse in Taunton.

I cherish the memories I have of standing on the terraces with my Dad cheering him on. Jimmy remains my hero. He is simply the greatest goalscorer ever.

WHEN THE ANGELS DESCENDED AT THE LANE

JOE LESLIE, London

Who can forget those magic names that are embedded forever in the memory of all of us who were lucky to see them? Brown - Baker - Henry - Blanchflower - Norman - Mackay- Jones - White - Smith - Allen - Dyson. I remember with a tingle how Danny was always first out on the pitch and he would kick the ball that he was carrying ... and then behind him, a regular routine, Dave Mackay hoofing the ball high and then trapping it as it came down. The support was sensational, and when the Double winners went marching into Europe they were accompanied by angels walking around the pitch with placards waved at the rival fans, reading: "The End of the World Is Nigh." This all to the chorused backgrounds of Glory Glory. What nights they were!

A STANDING OVATION AT THE FOREST

DENNIS BEESON, Kent

I was born midway between Tottenham and Arsenal, and as a young boy – along with my friends – I went to both Tottenham and Arsenal home games. The rivalry then was not as bitter as it seems to be today. However, because the first professional game I watched in 1948 – when I was 10 – was Blackpool v Tottenham in the FA Cup semi final I was to become a lifelong Spurs supporter.

I am warmed by lots of memories, particularly of the performances of David Mackay. He remains my all-time hero, and in my opinion he rates as the best all-round footballer there has ever been.

My most outstanding memories of the Double Season are:

Spurs playing Forest in Nottingham where Spurs were just about perfect. The *Sunday People* reporter, Ralph Finn, marked every player 10 out of 10, and the team got a standing ovation from the sporting Forest supporters. I was at the match and my lasting memory is of Mackay and Terry Dyson emerging from the tunnel for the second-half, both smoking cigarettes. This didn't seem to affect their fitness and contribution to this outstanding performance by our team.

My second memory is from the following season when Spurs beat Glasgow Rangers 5-2 with a magnificent exhition of football. Rangers also had fantastic players like Willie Henderson and Jim Baxter, but they could not live with Tottenham that day. It

Cliff Jones, one of the world's great wingers, appears to be looking up to planet football

is not only the football that has remained in my memory. I got hit over the head with a bottle by a female Glasgow Rangers supporter who was not best pleased with the way her team was taken apart. This was my first experience of football violence.

THE MEMORABLE MOMENT WHEN MY MOTHER FAINTED

STUART ELLISON, Sydney, Australia

I am currently living in Sydney Australia and have been a Spurs fan for over 50 years. My parents were 'Spurs mad' and season ticket holders. At aged five, they took me to my first live game which just happened to be Bill Nicholson's first game in charge – the famous 10-4 win over Everton in October 1958. What an introduction to the Mighty Spurs! Being so young I didn't know whether this was a typical scoreline.

From then on I went to every game with my parents, including the 2-0 FA Cup final win against Leicester City. We'd won the League and Cup, something no other team had achieved that century. My mother was so excited that when the final whistle blew she fainted, and her concerned young son tugged on his father's arm to alert him to what had happened. His initial response, showing little empathy, was to quickly glance down and then continue celebrating, yelling: "What do you expect? We've just won the Double." Only then did he go to her aid.

Looking back, it was a funny incident that has long been etched in my memory and a story I have told many times over the years. It is part of our family folklore.

We remained season ticket holders until 1969 before moving Down Under. I felt privileged to be able to watch, in my opinion, the most exciting era of the game. I still follow all the Spurs games live on TV here in Oz and have managed to see a few games live on the times I've been back to the UK. But there will never be anything to beat that Double year.

THE PERFECT ENGINE ROOM

ALAN PAPWORTH, London

Oh to be 10 years older – I would have seen and appreciated the swinging 60's more, the best decade ever for a young man but that's another story. I did not start going to see Spurs until 1965 but was well aware of the greatness of the Double team from a young age and have the benefit of having known people who had the pleasure of seeing what was arguably one of the best club sides ever. The overiding memory I get is that the team was built around three brilliant players in the engine room of the midfield, with the rest of the team blending perfectly together for a sublime period of about four years until age took its toll on Danny Blanchflower, the double broken leg of Dave Mackay and the tragic early death of John White. They were three irreplacable players. What must have Bill Nicholson felt to lose those three Lane legends within the space of year?

BILL NICHOLSON ON THE IMPORTANCE OF TEAM SPIRIT

HENRY JONES, Scarborough

The memory that most warms me in the autum of my years is sharing a train journey to Scarborough from London with Bill Nicholson, and I always thank the Gods who sat him next to me. He was on his way to his hometown for a family occasion just a few seasons after the Tottenham Double. I had witnessed virtually every home game while studying at London University. I am sure that Mr Nicholson would have jumped off the train if he had realised he was stuck next to a Spurs nut, but he proved marvellous company and was quite happy to talk about the team and that Double season in particular. What stands out most from the conversation was how he was equally effusive about the "lesser" stars of the side, and continually stressed the importance of it being a *team* triumph. He built a team spirit at White Hart Lane on which you could warm your hands. It is good to see Harry Redknapp also brining this spirit to the side, because a team is half as effective without that all-important camaraderie.

BORN TO SUPPORT 'TIP-TOP TOTTENHAM HOTSPUR'

ALAN FITTER, Hackney

As the 1960-61 season began I was in my last year as a 'tweenager' although I don't think we were called that back then and awaiting the onset of pubescent acne – which luckily never arrived which was odd as I was born in 'Ackney (there's a joke in there somewhere – I think).

I'd been a Spurs supporter since birth following in the footsteps of my Dad and my Grandfather who had lived in Tottenham after leaving the East End in the thirties. My Dad worked as a hairdresser in Stamford Hill so couldn't get to games on a Saturday as he had to work, so I'd go with my Uncle Frank and occasionally with my cousin Michael. We'd stand in either the enclosure (which is where the lower West Stand is now) and had a superb view or in the Pensioner's Enclosure. I've no idea why it was called that as anyone could stand in there and it was a little cheaper than the rest of the ground – I think it was one shilling and sixpence (seven and a half pence in our new fangled decimal currency). I can only think it was cheaper to encourage the over 65's and also it was right in the corner of the East and South Stands approximately where the drummer sits these days (although I don't think he's been there much recently).

So I was privileged to go to most, if not all the home matches that memorable season (I wasn't allowed to go to any away games – and I didn't have the money anyway). Those old black and white newsreels can't do justice to the brand of attacking football we played and although it's been repeated so many times that it's become a cliché, on muddy, grassless pitches (well after about November) kicking and heading a heavy leather football that absorbed moisture and big clod-hopper boots.

We got off to an amazing start to the season, and it was obvious that history was in the making. It's hard to describe how good we were – you had to have been there – but to watch the likes of Dave Mackay, Danny Blanchflower, John White and Cliff Jones crush the opposition week after week was a joy for a 12-year-old standing often in the freezing cold on the crumbling terraces with just a cup of hot Bovril for sustenance.

My Dad couldn't get to Saturday games but he could get to those in mid-week. Now when I say 'could' it meant he wasn't working but he didn't like standing and tickets for the seats were difficult, if not impossible to get on a match-by-match basis – but he had a secret weapon. His best friend, a wonderful man called Dave Starr, had a children's clothing factory on the Wingate Estate right next to the ground.

Dave liked the odd drink or three and used to spend his lunchtimes in the pub next to the ground on the corner of what is now Bill Nicholson Way and the High Road. Incredibly it was where the players spent many a lunchtime after they had been training either on the White Hart Lane pitch (when it wasn't too muddy) or in the ball court which was sadly demolished a few years ago to extend the car park.

Dave got friendly with a number of the players, so much so that the following year when I had my bar-mitzvah (I was a Yid before we were all called that), Dave arranged for Cliff Jones, Terry Medwin and Bobby Smith to attend the party (I have the photos to prove it). Not only did Dave befriend the players but he got to know the man in the ticket office, whose name if I remember correctly was Bill Beeby and Bill used to sort them out tickets when he could. However, I don't think he could help them for every match and there may have been occasions when dodgy transactions were done with Johnny The Stick who was the precursor of Stan Flashman in the ticket brokering world – or as they were called then 'those poxy touts'!

As I was saying, I had gone to every home game and the Championship was coming our way. The big game was on Wednesday April 17th when we due to play Sheffield

Bar-Mitzvah Boy Alan Fitter's scrapbook memories. He is pictured here with his Tottenham Hotspur heroes Terry Medwin (left) Cliff Jones (centre) and Bobby Smith (right).

Wednesday who were our only real rivals and lying second in the table – a win that night would mean that the Championship was ours. An enormous crowd was expected and tickets were at a premium and Dave could only get two. It meant that I would have to stand, but that was ok and was really looking forward to it when the bombshell landed – I wasn't allowed to go!

My parents were worried that the enormous scrum of people queuing all day to get on to the terraces would be too much for a very small 12-year-old and that I would be crushed. My crying and gnashing of teeth failed to persuade them and I had to stay at home that night. My Dad and Dave went and because they planned to get there early, Dave was put in charge of the provisions and brought some sandwiches. Well, the crowd trying to get in was enormous and although they had tickets, they were hemmed in on all sides as they made their way towards the West Stand stairs.

Dave delighted in telling everyone for years about the police horse that stood on his toe and almost broke it – it was his badge of courage for a long time! When they finally got into the ground, my Dad was starving and asked Dave for one of the sandwiches, only to find that although Dave was still tightly clutching in rigid fingers the top of the paper bag, the bottom and all its contents had been lost somewhere in the crowd – maybe the horse who trod on his toe got to eat them? They were probably right not to have let me go (I think I've finally forgiven them after 49 years) as the 'reported' crowd inside was 62,000 (and was probably more than that) – and there were tens of thousands locked outside.

So I'd missed the most important game of the season, but we won it 2-1 with goals from Smith and Allen and we were Champions for the second time in our history and were in the European Cup the following season. To make up for my disappointment, Dave got me a seat in the West Stand for the last game of the season against West Brom. We needed just a point to break the all-time League points record but with the Cup final just a week away (no squad rotation then), we were a bit flat and lost 1-2. After the final whistle, the players went into the dressing-room but the crowd refused to leave and chanted for ages for the team to come back out. Finally our heroes made their way to the front of the Director's Box but it obviously wasn't my day because from where I was sitting and being quite small, I couldn't see a thing!

But even that little disappointment on that sunny April day couldn't detract from the fact that I had been able to see week-after-week, one of the best teams in the history of English football strut their stuff – and I do mean strut. And it was made even better during the following week when without the help of Bill Beeby or Johnny The Stick, my Dad came up trumps and got me a standing ticket behind the goal for the Cup final and I was incredibly fortunate to be at Wembley to see us do 'the double' and cement our reputation as 'Super Spurs' – or as that cheesy song by The Tottenhamites proclaimed 'Tip Top Tottenham Hotspur'.

FINNEY PUT ME ON A FUNNY PATH TO TOTTENHAM
TOM RIMMER, Newton Longville, Bucks
I have an early memory of Spurs which, strictly, is pre-double year. I was born (1950) and bred in Southport, and from an early age went religiously to Haig Avenue to support the Sandgrounders who were then in the Fourth Division. As a nine-year old, early in 1960, my father took me to Deepdale as a treat to watch Preston, who were then in the First Division. I think the reason for the trip was two-fold – firstly to experience a premier division match and secondly to get to watch Tom Finney in the flesh before he retired. My Dad was a big Tom Finney fan.

Anyway, the opponents at Deepdale that day were a bunch of Southern softies called Tottenham Hotspur! Well, I was in awe of the way Spurs played from the off. Push and run, pass and move, call it what you will, it was 90 minutes of a smooth passing game that was completely alien to a young lad brought up on a Fourth Division diet of lump it and hope.

The Spurs team that day was virtually the double-winning side of the following season – the only absentee was Dave Mackay with Tony Marchi deputising for him. The names still roll off the tongue – Brown, Baker, Henry, Blanchflower, Norman, Marchi, Jones, White, Smith, Allen and Dyson. However, the man who stole the show for me was John White, and I can only regard myself as very fortunate to have had the opportunity of seeing him play live.

My memories of the match itself are sketchy to say the least. The result was 1-1 and I don't recall the scorers. I do recall a young wing-half playing for Preston by the name of Tommy Docherty. However, I was hooked!

That trip to Preston changed the course of my football supporting life. I was a Spurs fan from that day on.

I still continued to support Southport, until I left the town. However, because of Southport's close affinity to Everton, I probably would have grown up as a Toffee had my Dad not taken me to see his hero, Tom Finney.

A GOLDEN MEMORY OF THE GUNNERS BEING SHOT DOWN

BRIAN BERG, London W1, Managing Director of Universal Music TV (UMTV)

I was lucky enough to go to White Hart Lane with my father from the age of eight (1958), so I was privileged to watch many of those great matches from that golden Double season.

One of my fondest memories was being taken by Dad to see Spurs play Arsenal at home; I think it was in September 1960. He said to me, "These games are really special and it's so important that we beat the team whose Highbury ground is just around the corner from us at our home."

We beat them 3-2, and like most North Londoners that experience 50 years ago is engraved in my memory!

Going to school round the corner to Arsenal was an interesting time as I couldn't boast too loudly about the silky skills of Danny Blanchflower and John White, the raw power of Dave Mackay and the greyhound pace of Cliff Jones.

I have never seen a team match the '61 Spurs side in terms of sheer quality and dominating football, as smooth as a Rolls Royce engine.

As I write this, Spurs have just beaten Arsenal 2-1, including a wonder goal from an unknown kid called Danny Rose. That again took me back down memory lane to when I saw us beat Arsenal half-a-Century ago in the never-to-be-forgotten Double year. What memories.

MARVELLING AT OUR GREAT HISTORY

ROBERT ROCKETT, Maidenhead

I was too young to appreciate what was going on in the Double year, but I've seen enough from videos and DVDs and by reading to know we can marvel at the great history of our club. 'Sir Bill' Nicholson had them playing cavalier football, and after the Double the team's greatest achievement must have been becoming the first British side to win a major European trophy in 1963. It might have come earlier but for a Danish linesman called Hensen and a tubby referee named Aage Poulsen. I know from watching the Glory Glory Nights that is was these two officials who combined to rule out a legitimate goal from Jimmy Greaves against Benfica in the 1962 European Cup semi-final. How different things might have been had they allowed that goal!

WHERE THERE'S A WILL THERE'S A WAY FOR SPURS

STEVE MILLINGTON, New Zealand via Southend-on-Sea

Although I was born in Southend-on-Sea in 1948, Mum had spent most of her life in the Tottenham area, and both Mum and Dad had always been Spurs supporters and so it has been a family thing.

My earliest recollections of Tottenham were in the late 1950s: on match days we all set off quite early from Southend and made our way to Tottenham Cemetery to attend to the family grave. Then, while Dad went to The Lane, Mum helped out behind the bar at the White Hart (Rudolph's now I believe). The publican's name, if I correctly recall was Sam Langford, whose wife was Mum's aunt. At first I was considered too young to accompany Dad to the game, so my first match-day memories were of watching the fans going along what is now 'Bill Nicholson Way' from an upstairs pub window.

I couldn't wait to join Dad at a game, and when the 60's came I did – up there on 'The Shelf' for what was an unbelievable start to my own 50-plus years as a supporter. We later became season-ticket holders and I could fill a book with my memories, not just of the Double Season, but of so much more since. The last 'big' game Dad and I attended was the UEFA Cup final second-leg when we beat Anderlecht in that dramatic penalty shoot-out. Dad died soon after, and I emigrated to New Zealand.

I still get home to The Lane on occasional trips back to London, and my 'final' trip is already planned: It is in my will, and my wife and children are well-instructed, that my ashes are to be taken to Tottenham Cemetery and scattered on the family grave, ideally while a match is in progress – the sound of the crowd carries that far.

Oh yes, and my treasured possession – along with all the old programmes, books and memorabilia, a pewter tankard with the engraved autographs of the 1960-61 Double Team!

EVEN BETTER THAN THE WORLD CUP!

MORRIS KESTON, whose remarkable story of watching Spurs play 3,000 times is superbly captured in SUPERFAN, a book he has written with Nick Hawkins (www.visionsp.co.uk)

The most memorable of all the FA Cup finals I have attended was in 1961, when Spurs clinched the Double. I was beside myself with joy. I had seen Spurs lose three semi-finals over a 13-year period, and this more than made up for the disappointments. By then I had watched countless games at Wembley, including eight FA Cup finals, but this time it was different. This time it was my beloved Tottenham at Wembley and about to create history.

Watching Danny Blanchflower lift the trophy aloft that day was the best feeling I've ever had in my many visits to Wembley, greater even then when my good friend Bobby Moore collected the Jules Rimet trophy from her Majesty the Queen in 1966.

HOW I BOUGHT A CUP TICKET FROM A TOUT IN A TOILET!

PATRICK MURPHY, Somerset

I was 12 years old when the season started. Although I lived in Leamington Spa, nearly 100 miles from White Hart Lane, Spurs were already my team and Danny Blanchflower my boyhood hero. My father first took me to see them win at West Brom on Easter Monday 1957 and I took myself by coach to Birmingham and by train to the crucial end of season game at Wolves, in 1959/60. At the start of the double season I started keeping a scrapbook of Spurs photographs and articles from newspapers and magazines, so I have my own boys record of the Double.

Despite my age I managed to travel, on my own, to see six matches - the League games at Wolves, West Brom, Aston Villa and Birmingham City and the FA Cup fifth round and semi-final games against Aston Villa and Burnley respectively, both at Villa Park. The Cup games were all ticket which clearly presented a young lad in the Midlands with a problem. My mother generously gave me some extra money to try and purchase a ticket for the Villa tie and I headed off on an early train.

Arriving at the ground I popped into the toilets near the Holte End to answer a call of nature and there, sorting out a fistful of tickets, was a tout. I think he took pity on my tender age when he named his price, so I had my ticket.

I was just as lucky for the semi-final. Spurs' opponents, Burnley, stayed in a Leamington town centre hotel, so a friend and I went there on the night before the game, autograph hunting. We were lucky enough to be invited into a lounge where Burnley were relaxing and all the players, manager Harry Potts and chairman Bob Lord happily signed our autograph books. But the real highlight was that a third signature hunter turned up too and he had a spare ticket for the game! No need to spend a penny the next morning!

Travelling to these games was by train and the Spurs team were usually on the one I took, wearing my blue and white bobble hat and carrying my white painted football rattle, which would presumably be an offensive weapon in the current day, Particularly exciting was the return trip because the players waited on the station platform, mingling with other passengers including autograph hunters such as myself. It was thrilling to get so close to them and fascinating to watch how they dealt with young fans. Some players would have a pushing mob in front of them. Dave Mackay wouldn't accept that though. He was notable for his great air of authority, bellowing at everyone in his rich accent to get into an orderly line, whilst Danny Blanchflower's aura and seniority and Peter Baker's more austere demeanor seemed to illicit a calm approach from everyone.

Supporting a football team at a young age is incredibly exciting for every generation. Fifty years ago Tottenham were not only successful but played a beautiful brand of exciting, attractive, flowing football. All crowds are biased to their own team but in the early sixties supporters were not segregated and there was never a fear of violence on the terraces or in the stand. Fans of all opposition clubs were appreciative of Tottenham's football and it gave me a really warm glow when good moves were applauded by the home crowds amongst which I stood.

Of course it's easy to be on top of the world when your team is winning and the six times I saw them live that year they won every time, despite playing away from White Hart Lane. In those matches they scored seventeen goals and only conceded four. Ot all seems like only yesterday!

ALL THE QUEUING WAS WORTHWHILE

MIKE JACOB, Enfield

So many memories come rushing back from that fantastic Double season. Tops for me are the 3-2 win over Arsenal at Highbury and beating Man Utd 4-1 at home. And I recall rushing home from work to get back in time to see the FA Cup quarter-final replay against Sunderland that we won 5-0.

In those days it was all pay at the turnstiles, and we used to happily queue for ages to get in to see the games. It was always worthwhile.

All these years on I especially remember going to the Royal before spending the rest of the night queing outside the ground to get tickets for the FA Cup semi-final at Villa Park and then the thrill of seeing us finally win on what we considered a jinx ground.

But top of all my memories was when when we were crowned champions after beating Sheffield Wednesday and running on to the pttch, joining in the chants for the players to come out. We went mad when Danny led the players into the main stand. I will never forget that night, or that wonderful season.

A PURE FOOTBALLING SIDE

STEPHEN WILLIAM COLLARD, Bekesbourne, Kent

I was twelve years old and at an impressionable age when I first started to follow Tottenham. I was so proud of them when they won the Double because they were *MY* team, always had been and always will be. My memories of them that season is of them playing really good open, passing football – on the attack all the time. They were a balanced team, with good defenders and a forward line that scored more goals than any other First Division team. Above all, they were a pure footballing side.

Bill Nicholson must take the credit for putting together an exceptional team that blended perfectly. For me, they were the dream team and still are. When I compare them with the modern teams I know my memory is not playing tricks when I say they were superior in every way.

MEMORIES FROM THE SHELF

JEFFREY GARET, *Belsize Park*

I first watched Spurs in 1953, and I was 18 at the start of the double season seven years later. In that extraordinary season I was lucky enough to see around 40 of the 49 games they played on the way to the historic League and Cup triumph.

A group of us stood in one of the best positions in the ground, at the front in the middle of The Shelf. We used to arrive at least two hours before the start of each game and always enjoyed the banter and build up. The price to stand was four shillings (20p). A wonderful season of unbelievable performances reached its climax at Wembley Stadium for the FA Cup final on May 6 1961. I was lucky enough to obtain a ticket through the club ballot and I stood behind the goal where Bobby Smith and Terry Dyson scored the goals. We Spurs fans were thrilled and proud to have watched a great team achieve the first Double of the century playing exceptional football.

We used to travel to away games on the same train as the players. On the way back, after they had their meal, the players used to mingle and chat to the supporters. You really felt close to them. My great hero was Danny Blanchflower. It was a magical season that even 50 years on is clear in my memory.

PUSH AND RUN AT THE DOUBLE

JOHN HAWKIN. Hereford, formerly Edmonton

I was lucky enough to see the Push and Run Spurs and the Double side. You would have had the perfect team by combining them: Ditchburn, Ramsey, Burgess, Blanchflower, Norman, Mackay, Jones, White, Smith, Duquemin, Medley. My favourite Spurs player of the period was at his peak between the two sides ... little Tommy Harmer, who could make a ball sit up and talk.

ORDINARY TO THE EAR, EXTRAORDINARY TO THE EYE

RICHARD EARLY, Sussex

What do you call six Englishmen, three Scots, a Welshman and an Irishman? The answer: one of the best football club sides ever. Is that hyperbole? Probably not. Consult the news media of the time. A month into the 1960/61 season journalists had run out of superlatives to describe their performances and had to start recycling them to keep up with Tottenham Hotspur's magnificent charge for the coveted Double.

But though the football was sublime the names on the team sheet were, in contrast, so ordinary: Brown, Baker, Henry, Blanchflower, Norman, Mackay, Jones, White, Smith, Allen, Dyson.

Of the three Scots only the name Mackay makes any concession to nationality. As for Brown and White, well, how common are they? Jones – ok you wouldn't get a gold star for guessing that's Welsh, but half the people from Wales are called Jones. The English names are common or garden. That only leaves Blanchflower. His name had to stand out. If he had been born with a more common Belfast name, so cussedly, wonderfully, independent of mind was he, you imagine he would have reached out into the ether at the moment of birth to claim something more eye-catching like… Blanchflower, for example.

But apart from the captain and club genius – all the other names are just so strikingly commonplace. Look at them on the page. Who could imagine that this bunch of names would grace the highest levels of football achievement, and fifty years on still roll off the tongue.

By what alchemy was this mixture of Celt and Anglo-Saxon blended into such a potent symphony? By alchemist-in-chief, Bill Nicholson, of course. He assembled the team, lovingly fitting the jigsaw pieces together to create that moving tableau, demanding the highest standards from them and getting the response he wanted. From the front of the terraces, when he assumed command in 1958, I watched with boyish wonder as the process unfolded before my eyes.

In truth, the four outfield Celts made the difference, sprinkling stardust all around. They were the creative heartbeat of the team. The English yeomen brought strength, stability. Held it all together. First class professionals to a man. As with the manager, Smith and Dyson also hailed from North Yorkshire. Baker and Henry were London boys and Allen was from just down the road in Dagenham. Big Maurice was a Norfolk lad. These days of course it's totally different. Players come from all over the world. Is it better now? Was it better then?

Who can say. It was just different then, that's all. Different times. It's a global world we inhabit now. But 50 years ago ten blokes with ordinary names and a wizard from Belfast with a bit of an attitude, surfed the crest of English football. Made a big splash in Europe. Became legends.

Tottenham were busy rewriting the record books on their way to becoming the first team of the 20th Century to complete the League and FA Cup Double. Sports statistician **Michael Giller** tells the story of the historic season, figuratively speaking:

115 goals in the First Division on the way to the championship, a Spurs record (Aston Villa with 128 goals set the all-time record in 1930-31)

31 victories in 42 games, a League record

16 away wins in 21 games, a League record

11 straight victories from start of season, a record

66 points equalling the record set by Arsenal in 1930-31

50 points in the first 29 League games, a record

11 games **without conceding a goal** (v Everton, Wolves, Nottingham Forest (home and away), Birmingham, Preston (home and away), West Ham (home and away), Manchester City and Fulham)

11 home and away doubles, equalling the record for beating 11 clubs twice (set by Man U 1956-57 and Wolves 1958-59)

28 goals, Bobby Smith, **23 goals**, Les Allen

15 goals, Cliff Jones, **13 goals**, John White

12 goals, Terry Dyson, **6 goals**, Danny Blanchflower

5 goals, Terry Medwin, **4 goals**, Dave Mackay

4 goals, Maurice Norman, **3 goals**, Fank Saul

1 goal, Peter Baker, **1** own goal

13 League games in which four or more goals were scored (v Blackburn 4-1, Man United 4-1, Aston Villa 6-2, Wolves 4-0, Nottm Forest 4-0, Newcastle United 4-3, Fulham 5-1, Birmingham City 6-0, Burnley 4-4, Blackburn Rovers 5-2, Arsenal 4-2, Chelsea 4-2, Preston 5-0)

Four players appeared in all 42 League games: Ron Henry, Danny Blanchflower, John White, Les Allen. Three missed just one match: Bill Brown, Peter Baker, Maurice Norman. Terry Dyson missed two matches

2,037,671 spectators watched their 42 League games

Six First Division matches at The Lane drew more than 60,000 spectators:

65,930 v West Ham United, December 24 1960

65,251 v Arsenal, January 21 1961

65,032 v Chelsea, March 31 1965

62,261 v Wolves, February 22 1961

61,356 v Aston Villa, September 24 1960

61,205 v Sheffield Wednesday, April 17 1961

475,455 spectators watched their seven FA Cup ties, including the final in front of a 100,000 crowd at Wembley on May 6 1961. The top attendance for an FA Cup tie at White Hart Lane was the quarter-final replay against Sunderland that drew **64,797** spectators

FA Cup scorers: **Five** Terry Dyson, **Five** Bobby Smith **Four** Les Allen, **Four** Cliff Jones, **Two** Dave Mackay, 1og

Ten players appeared in all seven FA Cup ties: Bill Brown, Peter Baker, Ron Henry, Danny Blanchflower, Maurice Norman, Dave Mackay, Bobby Smith, Les Allen, Terry Dyson. Cliff Jones missed one match, with Terry Medwin deputising.

In the first half of the season Tottenham scored **21** more goals and collected **10** more points than in the second half, and they won **5** more games

Lowest home attendance: **35,753** v Nottingham Forest on April 26 1961, a week after clinching the Championship against Sheffield Wednesday.

● Tottenham's players were superstitious about the order in which they ran on to the pitch. Danny Blanchflower always came out first with a ball balanced on his right hand, goalkeeper Bill Brown had to be second and Maurice Norman was always last. John White insisted that Cliff Jones had to be behind him. Dave Mackay always kicked the ball high above him as he stepped on to the pitch, and would then trap it dead.

● To give the season a real Tottenham tinge, former White Hart Lane favourites Alf Ramsey and Arthur Rowe were also celebrating ... Alf led Ipswich to promotion as Second Division champions and Arthur steered Crystal Palace from the Fourth to Third Division. Spurs reserves were runners-up to Chelsea in the Combination league and the third team raced away with the Eastern Counties championship.

● Spurs wiped out a jinx when they beat Burnley 3-0 in the FA Cup semi-final at Villa Park. This was the ground where they had been beaten in the 1948, 1953 and 1956 FA Cup semi-finals.

● Forty-eight hours before the FA Cup final, Danny Blanchflower collected his second Footballer of the Year award from the Football Writers' Association.

● Bill Nicholson became the first man to win the League championship with the same club as player and manager.

● Perfectionist Danny Blanchflower insisted on havng ten pairs of boots to choose from, selecting only after a thorough pitch inspection and weighing up the conditions.

● People seeing the Tottenham team coach leaving Hillsborough after their first defeat of the seaon by Sheffield Wednesday in their 17th match were astonished to see and hear the Spurs players singing their heads off. "We felt as if a weight had been lifted off our shoulders," explained Maurice Norman. "Now we did not have to worry about losing, just about winning."

● The White Hart Lane gates were locked behind 64,797 fans for the FA Cup quarter-final replay against Sunderland. Among the thousands shut out was Bobby Smith! He was forced to abandon his car and thumb a lift with a police motorcyclist, who got him to the ground twenty minutes before the kick-off.

● Les Allen was fretting over the injury to Len Chalmers in the FA Cup final at the after-match victory banquet. He was feeling guilty that his tackle had caused the injury, even though it had been an accident. Les cheered up when a telegram was delivered to him at the Savoy Hotel. It read: "Forget about it. Congratulations. Len Chalmers."

● Bill Nicholson, who earned just £1,500 in that Double season, was presented with an electric shaver as a whip-round 'thank you' present from his players.

● Each Spurs player received a set of suitcases from the club along with a small cash bonus in keeping with League regulations. Ron Henry, who averaged £16 a week, put his bonus down as a deposit on a Vauxhall Victor car that he bought on hire purchase. The £20 a week maximum wage was kicked out the next season.

EXTRA-TIME: *After the Ball*

What Happened Next for the Heroes ...

Super Spurs, strengthened by the arrival of Jimmy Greaves from AC Milan, retained the FA Cup with a 3-1 victory over Burnley in the 1962 final, reached the semi-final of the European Cup where they were beaten in controversial circumstances by Benfica, and in 1963 became the first British club to win a major European trophy when they beat holders Atletico Madrid 5-1 in the Cup Winners' Cup final in Rotterdam. Then the break up of Bill Nicholson's dream team began...

BILL BROWN continued as Tottenham's reliable last line of defence for three years until making way for a promising young import from Watford called Pat Jennings. He shared the goalkeeping duties with the inexperienced Irishman until moving to Northampton Town in 1966. The following year he joined Toronto Falcons, and settled down to a new life in Canada. He worked for a Toronto property developer before joining the Ontario Land Department in 1975. He died after a lengthy illness on December 1 2004, aged 73.

PETER BAKER made way for Cyril Knowles, signed from Middlesbrough in 1964. Unlucky to be the only member of the Double defence not capped, he emigrated to South Africa, contnuing his football career as player-manager in Durban before setting up a successful office furniture and stationery business. Still a regular visitor to The Lane when visiting his old Enfield haunts.

RON HENRY was forced to surrender his first-team place in 1966 by a recurring knee injury but continued to play for the reserves while coaching the youth team. He combined coaching with running a 14-acre market garden near his home in Redbourne, Hertfordshire, where he followed his hobby of keeping homing pigeons. His grandson, Ronnie Henry, became the first captain to lift a trophy at the new Wembley Stadium when playing for Stevenage Borough.

DANNY BLANCHFLOWER reluctantly hung up his boots in the spring of 1964 at the age of 38, giving in to a knee problem that haunted him throughout the final years of his playing career. He became a widely read columnist with *The Observer* and then the *Sunday Express* and – after failing to land the Tottenham manager's job in 1974 – made a brief return to the game as manager of the Northern Ireland team. In 1978 he took charge at Chelsea for nine unhappy months before resigning – jumping before he was pushed. Danny became a vicitm of Alzheimer's, passing away in a Surrey nursing home at the age of 67.

MAURICE NORMAN suffered a horrific broken leg in a meaningless friendly against a Hungarian XI in 1965, an injury that effectively finished his career although it was two years before he finally threw in the towel. Mike England was brought in as a replacement, and the unfortunate Norman lost his chance of playing in the 1966 World Cup. After working in a garage business and owning a wool shop, green-fingered Maurice returned to his native Norfolk and to his first love of gardening.

DAVE MACKAY recovered from two broken legs to steer Spurs as skipper to the 1967 FA Cup final triumph over Chelsea. Brian Clough persuaded him to join Derby County in 1968, cleverly switching him from midfield to a steady role alongside centre-half Roy McFarland at the heart of the Derby defence. He helped the Rams take the Second Division championship in his first season at the Baseball ground, and shared the FWA Footballer of the Year award with Man City's Tony Book. He wound down his playing career as player-manager of Swindon before returning to Derby as manager in 1972, capturing the League title in his second season as successor to the controversial Cloughie. Dave the Brave briefly took over as manager of Walsall before coaching in the Middle East with great success between short spells in charge at Doncaster Rovers and Birmingham City. He wound down his coaching career in Qatar before retiring in 1997 and returning to live in the Midlands.

CLIFF JONES was on the Tottenham substitute's bench for the 1967 FA Cup final, the first time that subs had been used at Wembley. He joined Fulham in 1968 at the age of 33, and later played non-League football with with Kings Lynn, Wealdstone, Bedford Town, Cambridge City and Leyton Wingate. Cliff worked as a Covent Garden porter before returning to the sheet metal-working world in which he had served an apprenticeship. He later played rugby union as – surprise, surprise – a flying winger, became a PE teacher at Highbury Grove School and with Holloway Boys in Arsenal territory. Cliff is a popular 'meeter and greeter' on match days in the Legends Lounge at White Hart Lane.

JOHN WHITE was tragically killed when struck by lightning on Crews Hill Golf Course, Enfield, on July 21 1964 at the age of 27. He was at the peak of his powers, and recognised throughout the game as the player who did most to make the Tottenham team tick. He was married to Sandra Evans, the daughter of Tottenham assistant manager Harry Evans, who had died from a heart attack just 20 months earlier. His son, Rob, who was a baby when his Dad died, is an accomplished photographer and has written a moving book about 'The Dad I Never Knew.'

BOBBY SMITH After the Double, Bobby had two barnstorming seasons alongside Jimmy Greaves before a succession of injuries started to slow him down. He moved on to Brighton in May 1964 for £5,000. Norman Giller writes: "I was interviewing Brighton manager Archie Macaulay when Bobby reported for pre-season training, and I arranged for *Daily Express* sports photographer Norman 'Speedy' Quicke to take a picture of Bobby weighing-in on the club scales. It was going to be just an innocent 'atmosphere' picture. Smithy had weighed 13st 9lbs according to the Spurs records. Archie Macaulay hit the roof when the arrow on the scales shot up to 16st 9lbs! It went from being a run-of-the-mill photo to supporting a back page lead story under the headline 'Blobby Smith!'" He was given extra training, and got himself in good enough shape to help shoot Brighton to the Fourth Division title before moving to Hastings for the final shots of his goal-gorged career. Bobby, who gambled away much of his money, became a painter and decorator and drove a minicab before the crippling injuries he had collected on the football field finally caught up with him. He had to take a disability pension after suffering heart problems and having a hip replacement. Bobby gets the hero worship he deserves when he attends matches at White Hart Lane and will always be remembered as the man who scored most goals in the historic Double season.

LES ALLEN eventually lost his place to Jimmy Greaves and when Alan Gilzean arrived from Dundee he transferred to Queens Park Rangers, where he became manager in 1968-69. In 1972 he followed Dave Mackay as manager at Swindon, staying for two years before quitting football to concentrate on his skill in model making and sharing his time between living in England and on his favourite island of Cyprus. From a family steeped in football, his links with the game continued through his sons Clive and Bradley and his nephews Martin and Paul. The association with Tottenham continues with Clive working in Harry Redknapp's backroom team as an enthusiastic and knowledgeable coach. Between them, Allen and Son gathered 173 goals for Spurs – Les 61, Clive 112.

TERRY DYSON joined Fulham in the summer of 1965 and then moved on to Colchester United in 1968 before winding down his career with non-League Guildford. He tried his hand at management with Dagenham and Boreham Wood and then became a PE teacher at Hampstead High School and helped out at a school for troubled youngsters. The Football Association called on his experienced eye to assess schoolboy matches. Whenever he returns to White Hart Lane supporters talk warmly of the night the big-hearted Yorkshireman did so much to help win the Cup-Winners' Cup in 1963 with his two cracking goals against Atletico Madrid in the final.

TERRY MEDWIN was unluckily the first of the Double squad to have his career virtually finished by injury when he broke a leg playing against a South African select side in Cape Town in 1963. He coached at Fulham, and later became assistant to John Toshack at Swansea, where he started his career in 1949. He played just enough games (14) to earn a League championship medal in the Double season and collected an FA Cup winners' medal in 1962. Terry lives in his homeland of Wales, and always gets a huge welcome on his visits to White Hart Lane.

TONY MARCHI was a thoughtful and constructive stand-in for Dave Mackay when the Scottish braveheart was battling back to fitness after twice breaking a leg. He was briefly captain but his career in the top-flight was ended by a serious injury picked up in a match against Liverpool at Anfield in 1964. Tony became player-manager of Cambridge City, playing just one game. He then had a single season in charge at Northampton in 1967-68 before starting a DIY decorating shop in Essex, and later working for a maintenance company. Tony will always be part of Tottenham football folklore for the way he stood in for injured and 'irreplaceable' Mackay in the 1963 European Cup-Winners' Cup final, giving a performance of such authority that the magic of Mackay was not missed.

At a glance – every game, every goal, every scorer

Bulldozing Bobby Smith was top scorer for the Double team with 28 First Division goals and five in the FA Cup. Here he is 50 years on, and fiercely proud of his remarkable record.

20 Aug 1960	Everton	White Hart Lane	2–0	50,393	Smith, Allen
22 Aug 1960	Blackpool	Bloomfield Road	3–1	27,656	Medwin, Dyson (2),
27 Aug 1960	Blackburn Rovers	Ewood Park	4–1	26,819	Smith (2), Allen, Dyson
31 Aug 1960	Blackpool	White Hart Lane	3–1	45,684	Smith (3)
03 Sep 1960	Manchester United	White Hart Lane	4–1	55,442	Smith (2), Allen (2)
07 Sep 1960	Bolton Wanderers	Burnden Park	2–1	41,565	White, Allen
10 Sep 1960	Arsenal	Highbury	3–2	59,868	Saul, Allen, Dyson
14 Sep 1960	Bolton Wanderers	White Hart Lane	3–1	43,559	Blanchflower (pen), Smith (2)
17 Sep 1960	Leicester City	Filbert Street	2–1	30,129	Smith (2)
24 Sep 1960	Aston Villa	White Hart Lane	6–2	61,356	Mackay, White (2), Smith, Allen, Dyson
01 Oct 1960	Wolverhampton W.	Molineux	4–0	52,829	Blanchflower, Jones, Allen, Dyson
10 Oct 1960	Manchester City	White Hart Lane	1–1	58,916	Smith
15 Oct 1960	Nottingham Forest	City Ground	4–0	37,248	Mackay, Jones (2), White
29 Oct 1960	Newcastle United	St James' Park	4–3	51,369	Norman, Jones, White, Smith

Date	Opponent	Venue	Score	Attendance	Scorers
02 Nov 1960	Cardiff City	White Hart Lane	3–2	47,605	Blanchflower (p), Medwin, Dyson
05 Nov 1960	Fulham	White Hart Lane	5–1	56,270	Jones (2), White, Allen (2)
12 Nov 1960	Sheffield Wednesday	Hillsborough	1–2	53,988	Norman
19 Nov 1960	Birmingham City	White Hart Lane	6–0	46,010	Jones (2), White, Smith (p), Dyson (2)
26 Nov 1960	West Brom Albion	The Hawthorns	3–1	39,017	Smith (2), Allen
03 Dec 1960	Burnley	White Hart Lane	4–4	58,737	Norman, Mackay, Jones (2)
10 Dec 1960	Preston North End	Deepdale	1–0	21,657	Smith
17 Dec 1960	Everton	Goodison Park	3–1	61,052	Mackay, White, Allen
24 Dec 1960	West Ham United	White Hart Lane	2–0	65,930	White, Dyson
26 Dec 1960	West Ham United	Upton Park	3–0	34,351	White, Allen, Brown (og)
31 Dec 1960	Blackburn Rovers	White Hart Lane	5–2	48,742	Blanchflower, Smith (2), Allen (2)
16 Jan 1961	Manchester United	Old Trafford	0–2	65,535	
21 Jan 1961	Arsenal	White Hart Lane	4–2	65,251	Blanchflower (pen), Smith, Allen (2)
04 Feb 1961	Leicester City	White Hart Lane	2–3	53,627	Blanchflower (pen), Allen

Date	Opponent	Venue	Score	Scorers
11 Feb 1961	Aston Villa	Villa Park	2–1	Smith, Dyson
22 Feb 1961	Wolverhampton W.	White Hart Lane	1–1	Smith
25 Feb 1961	Manchester City	MaineRoad	1–0	Medwin
11 Mar 1961	Cardiff City	Ninian Park	2–3	Allen, Dyson
22 Mar 1961	Newcastle United	White Hart Lane	1–2	Allen
25 Mar 1961	Fulham	Craven Cottage	0–0	
31 Mar 1961	Chelsea	White Hart Lane	4–2	Jones (2), Saul, Allen
01 Apr 1961	Preston North End	White Hart Lane	5–0	Jones (3), White, Saul
03 Apr 1961	Chelsea	Stamford Bridge	3–2	Norman, Smith, Medwin
08 Apr 1961	Birmingham	St Andrews	3–2	White, Smith, Allen
17 Apr 1961	Sheffield Wednesday	White Hart Lane	2–1	Smith, Allen
22 Apr 1961	Burnley	Turf Moor	2–4	Baker, Smith
26 Apr 1961	Nottingham Forest	White Hart Lane	1–0	Medwin
29 Apr 1961	West Brom Albion	White Hart Lane	1–2	Smith

Attendances: 50,786; 62,261; 40,278; 45,463; 46,470; 38,536; 65,032; 46,325; 57,103; 40,961; 61,205; 28,991; 35,753; 52,054

At a glance – every Cup tie, every goal, every scorer

Jet-paced Cliff Jones scored four goals on the way to Wembley. Here he is 50 years on, and a huge favourite at White Hart Lane when visiting the Legends Lounge.